# A BRIEF HISTORY OF BEN FRANKLIN FOR KIDS

Lightning, Letters, and Liberty: The Ingenious Life of America's Renaissance Man

SCOTT MATTHEWS

# Contents

| | |
|---|---|
| Introduction | vii |
| 1. Foundations of a Genius | 1 |
| 2. The Self-Made Man | 9 |
| 3. Pioneering Scientific Exploration | 25 |
| 4. Advocate for Unity and Education | 35 |
| 5. Diplomatic Endeavors and Political Strides | 44 |
| 6. Architect of Independence | 60 |
| 7. The Enduring Legacy | 70 |
| Conclusion | 77 |
| Appendices | 79 |
| References | 99 |

Copyright © 2024 Scott Matthews

All rights reserved. No part of this publication may be reproduced, distributed, or transmitted in any form or by any means, including photocopying, recording, or other electronic or mechanical methods, without the prior written permission of the publisher, except in the case of brief quotations embodied in critical reviews and certain other non-commercial uses permitted by copyright law.

Trademarked names appear throughout this book. Rather than use a trademark symbol with every occurrence of a trademarked name, names are used in an editorial fashion, with no intention of infringement of the respective owner's trademark. The information in this book is distributed on an "as is" basis, without warranty. Although every precaution has been taken in the preparation of this work, neither the author nor the publisher shall have any liability to any person or entity with respect to any loss or damage caused or alleged to be caused directly or indirectly by the information contained in this book.

*"Reading was the only amusement I allowed myself."*

*- Benjamin Franklin*

# Introduction

Embarking on the journey of chronicling Benjamin Franklin's life in *A Brief History of Ben Franklin for Kids - Lightning, Letters, and Liberty: The Ingenious Life of America's Renaissance Man* reveals a figure whose contributions profoundly shaped the course of history. This book is a tribute to a man who embodied the spirit of the Enlightenment and the founding ideals of the United States.

Benjamin's transformation from a young printer's apprentice to one of history's most influential figures is a testimony to his unquenchable curiosity and relentless drive for self-improvement. His journey, from humble beginnings in Boston to becoming a renowned scientist, diplomat, inventor, and statesman, underscores the power of perseverance and the pursuit of knowledge.

The narrative captures the essence of Benjamin's multi-dimensional life, interweaving his scientific discoveries, political achievements, and personal experiences. This detailed, chronological account aims to provide a comprehensive understanding of Benjamin's legacy and his profound impact on the formation of the United States and the broader world.

A remarkable aspect of Benjamin's life is his ability to bridge theory and practice. Whether experimenting with electricity, drafting the Declaration of Independence, or establishing the first public library,

Benjamin consistently applied intellectual insights to practical problems, enhancing the lives of those around him. His inventions, such as the lightning rod and bifocals, exemplify how his innovative spirit left a lasting mark on everyday life.

Benjamin's diplomatic endeavors, particularly his efforts to secure French support during the American Revolution, highlight his strategic thinking and perseverance. His charm, wit, and intellect made him an effective diplomat, apt at navigating the complexities of international relations and securing crucial alliances. These successes were instrumental in the triumph of the American cause.

Moreover, Benjamin's commitment to social justice and education stands out as a defining feature of his legacy. His role in founding the University of Pennsylvania, advocating for the removal of slavery, and establishing the Library Company of Philadelphia reflect his belief in the transformative power of knowledge and the importance of equality. These values continue to inspire and guide contemporary society.

*A Brief History of Ben Franklin for Kids* aims to provide readers with a deeper appreciation of Benjamin's legacy and the enduring impact of his contributions. His life serves as a powerful reminder of what can be achieved through curiosity, hard work, and a steadfast commitment to the common good. Benjamin's story is not merely a historical account; it is a source of inspiration, urging all to strive for greatness and make a positive difference in the world.

# 1. Foundations of a Genius

Benjamin Franklin, a figure of immense importance in American history, was born on January 17, 1706, in Boston, Massachusetts. His early life was shaped by a blend of familial expectations, a thirst for knowledge, and a motivation that would eventually lead him to become one of the most influential Founding Fathers of the United States.

Benjamin's father, Josiah Franklin, was a man of considerable resilience and versatility. He was born on December 23, 1657, in Ecton, Northamptonshire, England. His parents were Thomas Franklin, who worked as a blacksmith and farmer, and Jane White. Josiah's early life in England was shaped by the skills and trades of his father, giving him a strong foundation in manual labor and practical trades.

In his professional life, Josiah initially took up the occupation of a tallow chandler, soaper, and candlemaker. A tallow chandler was a person who made and sold candles from tallow, which is a type of rendered animal fat. This job was essential in a time when candles were the primary source of lighting. In addition to candle making, Josiah also made soap, which was another crucial commodity for households. His work as a candlemaker involved not only crafting the candles but also ensuring the quality and consistency of the tallow to produce a steady, reliable light.

Josiah Franklin's personal life was marked by two significant marriages. His first marriage was to Anne Child, with whom he had seven children. The couple emigrated from England to Boston in 1683, seeking better opportunities in the New World. Sadly, Anne Child passed away after a prolonged illness, leaving Josiah a widower with several young children to care for.

On July 9, 1689, Josiah married Abiah Folger in the Old South Meeting House in Boston. Abiah was born on August 15, 1667, in Nantucket, Massachusetts Bay Colony. She was the daughter of Peter Folger, a miller and schoolteacher, and Mary Morrell Folger, a former servant. The Folger family had a strong Puritan* background, and Peter Folger was known for his rebellious spirit and commitment to religious freedom. This heritage likely influenced Abiah's values and upbringing.

Together, Josiah and Abiah Franklin had ten children, adding to Josiah's seven from his first marriage, bringing the total number of children to seventeen. Benjamin Franklin was the fifteenth of these children and the eighth of the ten children born to Josiah and Abiah. Growing up in such a large family, Benjamin's early life was undoubtedly filled with the bustling activity and responsibilities that came with being part of a sizable household.

---

\* Puritans were a group of English Protestants in the late 16th and 17th centuries who sought to "purify" the Church of England from what they perceived as corrupt practices and doctrines inherited from the Roman Catholic Church. They believed in a strict moral code, simplicity in worship, and a personal, direct relationship with God without the need for an elaborate church hierarchy. The Puritans emphasized the importance of reading the Bible, personal piety, and living a life that reflected their religious beliefs. Many Puritans emigrated to the American colonies, seeking religious freedom and the opportunity to establish communities governed by their religious principles. Their influence was significant in shaping the social, political, and religious landscape of early American society.

The Franklin family's household in Boston was a lively and industrious environment. Josiah's work as a tallow chandler, soaper, and candlemaker provided the family with a stable, though modest, income. Despite financial limitations, Josiah and Abiah were determined to provide their children with opportunities to learn and grow. This commitment to education and hard work would greatly influence Benjamin's character and future achievements.

From a young age, Benjamin Franklin demonstrated a strong sense of leadership and curiosity. He was "generally the leader among the boys," often organizing activities and engaging in various experiments that showcased his inquisitive mind and inventive spirit. Whether it was leading games, constructing makeshift devices, or simply exploring the world around him, Benjamin's early years were marked by a natural propensity for leadership and a thirst for knowledge.

Recognizing Benjamin's potential, his father, Josiah Franklin, harbored hopes of providing his son with a formal education that would prepare him for a career in the clergy. This aspiration was fueled by the belief that a learned and pious life was one of the highest callings. Consequently, Benjamin was enrolled in Boston Latin School, a prestigious institution known for its rigorous academic curriculum designed to prepare young boys for college and, ultimately, the ministry.

Benjamin's time at Boston Latin School, however, was short-lived. Although he excelled in his studies and showed great promise, the family's financial constraints soon became a limiting factor. Josiah, despite his industriousness and multiple trades, could not afford the ongoing costs of a formal education for his children. The economic reality of maintaining a large household with seventeen children meant that resources were stretched thin.

After just two years at Boston Latin School, Benjamin's formal education came to an abrupt end when he was ten years old. This decision was driven by the immediate need for additional hands in the family business of candle and soap making. Although this work was far from intellectually stimulating, it was necessary for the family's survival. Young Benjamin joined his father in the workshop, where he learned the trades of tallow chandler, soaper, and candlemaker.

Despite the end of his formal schooling, Benjamin's education did not cease. His curiosity and passion for learning continued to drive him. He became a voracious reader, seeking knowledge from any books he could find. His father's modest library, coupled with borrowed books from friends and local collections, became his primary source of education. Benjamin would often read late into the night, absorbing a wide range of subjects from literature and science to philosophy and politics.

In addition to his self-directed reading, Benjamin also honed his writing skills. He practiced composing essays and letters, mimicking the styles of the authors he admired. This self-education laid the foundation for his later success as a writer and publisher.

Around this age, Benjamin Franklin also began to grapple with the complexities and dilemmas of religion. While his father Josiah followed strict Puritan teachings, his mother Abiah came from a family that had fled such rigidity. This contrast in his upbringing played a crucial role in shaping Benjamin's religious perspectives.

Abiah, who had experienced the oppressive nature of strict Puritanism, instilled in her children a more unorthodox approach to religious education. This likely contributed to Benjamin's early questioning and exploration of faith. Unlike the conventional Puritan emphasis on rigidity in following principles, Abiah's teachings encouraged a more open-minded and reflective approach. This environment allowed Benjamin to develop a nuanced understanding of religion, one that was not confined to the dogmatic constraints of his father's Puritanism.

At the age of twelve, recognizing that Benjamin's intellectual talents were not being fully utilized in the family business, Josiah arranged for him to become an apprentice to his older son, James Franklin, who was a printer. This apprenticeship would prove to be a turning point in Benjamin's life. The printing trade offered a unique blend of manual labor and intellectual engagement, allowing him to combine his practical skills with his love of learning.

Under James's study, Benjamin learned the intricacies of typesetting, printing, and publishing. The world of print opened up new opportunities for him to explore his interests and talents. Working with printed materials every day, Benjamin had access to a wealth of information and ideas, further fueling his intellectual curiosity. He read widely, wrote frequently, and began to develop his own views on a variety of subjects.

During his apprenticeship, Benjamin's talent for writing began to shine. At the age of fifteen, he secretly contributed to his brother's newspaper, *The New-England Courant*, using the pseudonym "Silence Dogood." The letters written by "Silence Dogood," a fictional middle-aged widow, were witty, insightful, and quickly gained popularity among the newspaper's readers. This early success in writing not only boosted Benjamin's confidence but also demonstrated his potential as a thinker and communicator.

Despite his growing skills and contributions, Benjamin's relationship with his brother James was strained. The apprenticeship was marked by frequent disagreements and conflicts. James's strict and often harsh treatment led Benjamin to seek ways to assert his independence. At the age of sixteen, when James was jailed for publishing material that was critical of the local government, Benjamin took over the newspaper, showcasing his ability to manage the business and stand up for the principles of free speech and press. During the period of his brother's imprisonment, which lasted for about a month, young Benjamin demonstrated remarkable maturity and leadership. His successful handling of the newspaper during this challenging time was a testament to his burgeoning talents and determination to uphold the values he believed in, setting the stage for his future endeavors in the realm of public service and media.

By the time Benjamin was seventeen, his relationship with James had become strained to the breaking point. In 1723, he left his apprenticeship without permission, effectively becoming a fugitive. He sought a fresh start in Philadelphia, a city that would eventually become his home and the center of his many endeavors.

Arriving in Philadelphia, Benjamin found work in various printing shops but soon realized that his ambitions required more than just employment. His industrious nature and sharp mind caught the attention of Pennsylvania Governor Sir William Keith, who promised to help Benjamin establish his own printing business. With this encouragement, Benjamin traveled to London to acquire the necessary printing equipment. However, upon arrival, he discovered that Keith's promises were empty, and he was left to fend for himself in a foreign city.

In London, Benjamin worked as a typesetter in a printer's shop in the bustling Smithfield area. This experience, while challenging, significantly broadened his horizons and exposed him to new ideas and technologies. Benjamin was eighteen years old during this transformative period, which began in 1724. It was during this time that he began to form connections with several individuals who would later play significant roles in his life.

One of the first people Benjamin befriended was James Ralph, a poet and writer. They met through mutual acquaintances within the literary and printing communities, and quickly formed a close friendship. Ralph was an ambitious young man, much like Benjamin, and their shared love for literature and writing solidified their bond. They often spent long evenings discussing their dreams, exchanging ideas, and collaborating on various literary projects. Ralph's friendship provided Benjamin with much-needed emotional support and intellectual companionship during his challenging stay in London. Their discussions were a source of inspiration and helped Benjamin hone his writing skills, which would later become one of his greatest strengths.

Another significant connection Benjamin made was with William Strahan, a prominent printer. They met through the broader printing community in London, where Benjamin's work as a typesetter brought him into contact with many experienced printers. Strahan, recognizing Benjamin's potential, became both a mentor and a friend. He introduced Benjamin to advanced printing techniques and the intricacies of the publishing business. This  relationship not only provided Benjamin with valuable technical knowledge but also helped him establish important professional networks that would benefit him throughout his career. Strahan's influence and connections in the printing industry later facilitated the publication of Benjamin's works in Britain, enhancing his international reputation.

During his time in London, Benjamin also went to various coffeehouses, which were popular meeting places for intellectuals, writers, and businessmen. It was in these lively establishments that he met Sir Hans Sloane, a renowned physician and collector. Their introduction came through Benjamin's interest in science and natural philosophy, subjects that were often discussed in these coffeehouses. Sir Hans Sloane, impressed by Benjamin's curiosity and intellect, invited him to his extensive library and collections. This exposure to a wealth of scientific knowledge and the broader world of intellectual inquiry deeply influenced Benjamin. Sloane's encouragement and the rich intellectual environment he fostered inspired Benjamin to pursue his scientific endeavors more vigorously upon his return to Philadelphia.

Benjamin's professional and personal networks continued to expand with his acquaintance with Thomas Denham, a successful merchant. They met through their mutual involvement in the commercial and printing communities. Denham recognized Benjamin's talents and offered him a lifeline when his prospects in London appeared bleak. Understanding Benjamin's situation and potential, Denham extended an offer of employment as a clerk, shopkeeper, and bookkeeper upon Ben's return to Philadelphia. This position provided Benjamin with financial stability and the opportunity to reestablish himself in the city. Denham's support was crucial in helping Benjamin transition back to life in America, where he would lay the groundwork for his subsequent successes.

Additionally, Benjamin's time in London brought him into contact with John Collins, a childhood friend from Boston who had also ventured to London. They reconnected and often engaged in intellectual debates and discussions, much as they had in their youth. Collins' presence in London provided a familiar and comforting link to Benjamin's past, while their continued intellectual exchanges furthered Benjamin's development as a thinker and writer.

These connections, forged during his challenging yet enriching time in London, played pivotal roles in Benjamin's life. They provided him with a support network, intellectual stimulation, and professional opportunities that were instrumental in shaping him for his future. After a year and a half in London, encouraged by the support of Thomas Denham, Benjamin returned to Philadelphia in 1726. This period, marked by both hardships and rich experiences, significantly shaped Benjamin's intellectual and professional development, laying a solid foundation for his later achievements as a printer, inventor, statesman, and one of the most influential figures in American history.

Benjamin's early years were marked by a relentless pursuit of knowledge and self-improvement. Despite limited formal education, he became a voracious reader and an avid experimenter. He was deeply influenced by the intellectual currents of the Enlightenment,* embracing its emphasis on reason, scientific inquiry, and the improvement of society through knowledge. This intellectual curiosity would later lead him to make significant contributions to various fields, including science, politics, and philosophy.

---

* The Enlightenment, also known as the Age of Enlightenment or the Age of Reason, was an intellectual and cultural movement that emerged in Europe during the late 17th and 18th centuries. It emphasized reason, logic, and empirical evidence as the primary sources of knowledge and authority, challenging traditional doctrines and dogmas upheld by religion and monarchies.

## 2. The Self-Made Man

Benjamin Franklin's return to Philadelphia marked the beginning of a transformative period in his life. With the support of Thomas Denham, a British Quaker merchant who had become a close friend and mentor during Benjamin's time in London, Benjamin was ready to make his mark on the city and beyond.

Upon his arrival in Philadelphia in 1726, when he was twenty years of age, Benjamin took up a position as a clerk in Denham's store. This job, though modest, provided him with stability and an opportunity to observe the business world from the inside. Benjamin's keen mind absorbed every detail, and he soon began to dream of his own ventures.

However, tragedy struck in 1727 when Denham passed away. This loss was a significant blow to Benjamin, both personally and professionally. Despite the setback, Benjamin's resilience shone through. He took on various printing jobs and soon found a new opportunity that would lay the foundation for his future success.

In 1727, at the age of twenty-one, Benjamin Franklin established the Junto, a collective of like-minded aspiring artists and tradesmen dedicated to self-improvement and community betterment. Modeled after the English coffeehouses Benjamin had frequently visited in London, which were hotbeds for the spread of Enlightenment ideas, the Junto became a forum for discussing contemporary issues. This group was instrumental in creating numerous organizations in Philadelphia.

The Junto, sometimes referred to as the Leather Apron Club, was composed of individuals from various trades and professions. Members included printers, surveyors, cabinetmakers, and other skilled workers. This diversity enriched the discussions and debates that took place, as each member brought unique perspectives and expertise to the table. Notable members of the Junto included William Parsons and Thomas Godfrey. William Parsons, initially a shoemaker, later became the Surveyor General of Pennsylvania, responsible for mapping and overseeing land surveys in the state. Thomas Godfrey, a glazier by trade, was also a mathematician who invented the first sextant in America, an instrument used for measuring angles, especially for navigation at sea.

Moreover, reading was a cherished activity within the Junto, yet books were both rare and expensive. To address this, the members initially pooled their own collections, creating a shared library. Benjamin articulated the concept in the words:

"I proposed that since our books were frequently referenced during our discussions, it would be convenient to have them all available in one place for consultation. By combining our books into a common library, we would all benefit from access to the entire collection, almost as if each of us owned all the books."

Despite this effort, the resources were insufficient. Benjamin then envisioned a subscription library, where members would contribute funds to collectively purchase books for shared use. This idea materialized as the Library Company of Philadelphia, founded in

1731 with a charter composed by Benjamin himself. This innovative model provided a sustainable way to expand access to knowledge and became a cornerstone of the community's intellectual life.

However, the Junto's meetings were characterized by a structured format, which included a series of questions designed to stimulate conversation and reflection. Topics ranged from morality and politics to science and philosophy. Members were encouraged to express their thoughts freely but were also expected to listen respectfully and consider opposing viewpoints. This practice not only fostered intellectual growth but also helped develop Benjamin's skills in diplomacy and persuasion.

In addition to its intellectual pursuits, the Junto engaged in various community improvement projects. Members organized initiatives to clean and pave the streets of Philadelphia, enhance public safety, and establish institutions such as the first lending library and the first fire department. These efforts reflected the group's commitment to practical solutions and collective action for the public good.

The influence of the Junto extended beyond its immediate circle, as members often brought new ideas and innovations to their respective trades and communities. The collaborative spirit and the emphasis on mutual aid and self-education exemplified by the Junto were integral to the development of a civic-minded society in colonial America.

Junto's legacy is evident in the many organizations and institutions that followed its example. The Library Company of Philadelphia, born from Benjamin's vision, became a model for public libraries across the nation. Its establishment marked a significant step toward democratizing access to information and fostering a culture of learning and inquiry.

After creating Junto, Benjamin's entrepreneurial spirit also led him to establish his own print shop in 1728 with a partnership with Hugh Meredith. The shop quickly became a hub of activity, producing a variety of printed materials, including

books, pamphlets, and newspapers. This venture marked the beginning of Benjamin's significant impact on the publishing world in Philadelphia. The following year, he became the publisher of *The Pennsylvania Gazette*, a newspaper that soon became one of the most influential publications in the American colonies. *The Gazette* provided Benjamin with a platform to advocate for various local reforms and initiatives through his printed essays and observations.

Benjamin's writings in *The Gazette* were instrumental in addressing social and political issues, ranging from public safety and education to civic responsibility and economic development. His ability to communicate complex ideas clearly and persuasively earned him a reputation as a thoughtful and influential voice in the community. His strategic use of the newspaper to promote public discussion and debate on important issues helped to foster a more informed and engaged citizenry in Philadelphia.

In addition to his editorial contributions, Benjamin was known for his sharp wit and keen observations. He often wrote under pseudonyms, such as Silence Dogood and Richard Saunders, allowing him to explore different viewpoints and critique societal norms with humor and irony. These writings further solidified his reputation as a brilliant and versatile thinker.

Over time, Benjamin's commentary and his skillful cultivation of a positive image as an industrious and intellectual young man earned him considerable social respect. His success in the printing business and his growing influence in public affairs laid the groundwork for his later achievements in science, diplomacy, and politics.

Despite achieving fame and success, Benjamin remained grounded in his humble beginnings. He consistently signed his letters with the unpretentious "B. Franklin, Printer," a testament to his enduring connection to his roots in the printing trade. This humility endeared him to many and highlighted his belief in the value of hard work and practical skills.

Benjamin's partnership with Meredith eventually dissolved, but his printing business continued to thrive. He expanded his operations, taking on apprentices and diversifying the types of printed materials produced, including books, pamphlets, and government documents.

His business acumen and innovative approach to printing played a crucial role in his financial success and his ability to pursue his many other interests and endeavors.

Amid his growing business ventures, Benjamin's personal life also began to take shape. When he was seventeen years old, he had proposed to fifteen year old Deborah Read while he was a boarder in the Read household. At the time, Deborah's mother, recently widowed and cautious about her young daughter's future, was hesitant to approve the marriage. Benjamin was preparing to travel to London at the request of Governor Keith and lacked financial stability, which further concerned Deborah's mother. As a result, she declined Benjamin's request to marry her daughter.

Benjamin's journey to London turned out to be a significant turning point. During his time abroad, he failed to maintain communication with Deborah and her family. This prolonged silence was interpreted by Deborah and her mother as a breach of his promises and a sign that he had moved on. Encouraged by her mother, Deborah eventually married John Rogers, a potter, on August 5, 1725.

Unfortunately, the marriage to Rogers quickly turned disastrous. John Rogers ran to Barbados with Deborah's dowry to escape his debts and avoid prosecution, leaving her abandoned and in a difficult situation. With Rogers' fate unknown and no formal dissolution of their marriage, Deborah was unable to remarry due to bigamy laws, which prohibited her from entering into another marriage. Bigamy laws, which were strictly enforced during that time, made it illegal for an individual to marry again while their spouse was still legally alive, regardless of the circumstances of abandonment or lack of contact. These laws were intended to uphold the sanctity of marriage and prevent any potential legal disputes over property and inheritance rights.

The implications of these laws were significant for women like Deborah. Without a formal declaration of Rogers' death or a legal divorce, Deborah was considered legally married to him. This left her in a state where she was still legally married but had no contact with her husband and was unable to move forward with her life or enter into a new legally recognized marriage. Such laws were particularly harsh on women, who were often left without social or financial support if their husbands disappeared or abandoned them. Similarly, Deborah's inability to remarry legally until she was certain of Rogers' death placed her in a precarious position both socially and economically.

This complex and troubled period in Deborah's life eventually led her back to Benjamin. When Benjamin returned to Philadelphia in 1726, their paths crossed once more. Despite the legal and emotional complications, their relationship was rekindled, and in 1730, they entered into a common-law marriage. At the time of marriage, Benjamin was twenty-four years old, and Deborah was twenty-two years old. A common-law marriage is a legally recognized marriage between two people who have not obtained a marriage license or had their marriage approved by a ceremony. Instead, the marriage is established by the couple's actions and their agreement to be married.

Deborah proved to be an indispensable partner in Benjamin's life. She managed the household affairs with remarkable efficiency, allowing Benjamin to devote more time and energy to his numerous business and intellectual pursuits. Her contributions were not limited to domestic matters; Deborah also played a significant role in the operations of Benjamin's printing business. She assisted with bookkeeping, customer relations, and even helped to manage the shop in Benjamin's absence. Her steadfast support and capable management were crucial to the success and stability of their enterprises.

The couple had two children together: Francis Folger Franklin, born in 1732, and Sarah Franklin, affectionately known as Sally, born in 1743. Tragically, Francis died of smallpox at the age of four, a loss that deeply affected both Benjamin and Deborah. Despite this heartache, they continued to provide a loving and nurturing environment for their daughter, Sally, who would grow up to be a central figure in Benjamin's later life.

In addition to their children, Benjamin also acknowledged an illegitimate son, William Benjamin, born around 1730 from an earlier relationship with an unknown woman. Benjamin took full responsibility for William's upbringing, ensuring he received a good education and opportunities for advancement. Deborah accepted William into their household and treated him as part of the family, despite the unconventional circumstances of his birth.

Among these personal happenings, one of Benjamin's most notable achievements during this period was the creation of *Poor Richard's Almanack*. First published in 1732 under the pseudonym Richard Saunders, the almanack\* quickly became one of the most popular and enduring publications of its time. It was an annual book filled with a variety of content that appealed to a broad audience, including weather forecasts, practical household tips, puzzles, and entertaining aphorisms.

The almanack's success can be attributed to Benjamin's ability to blend practical information with humor and wisdom. Each edition was carefully crafted to provide useful advice and entertainment, making it a valuable resource for readers from all walks of life. The weather forecasts were particularly important in an era when accurate weather predictions were hard to come by, helping farmers and sailors plan their activities.

Benjamin's *Poor Richard's Almanack* was also known for its memorable and often humorous sayings, which were designed to impart practical wisdom and moral lessons. Phrases like "Early to bed and early to rise, makes a man healthy, wealthy, and wise" and "A penny saved is a penny earned" became widely quoted and are still

---

\* An almanack was a book containing a calendar of days, weeks, and months and usually facts about the rising and setting of the sun and moon, changes in the tides, and information of general interest.

recognized today. These aphorisms encapsulated Benjamin's practical approach to life and his belief in the virtues of hard work and self-improvement.

The almanack also included a variety of other content that catered to the interests and needs of its readers. Practical household tips offered advice on everything from cooking and farming to health and hygiene. Puzzles and riddles provided entertainment and mental stimulation, while stories and essays explored themes of morality, ethics, and human nature.

Benjamin's use of the pseudonym Richard Saunders allowed him to adopt a persona that could speak directly to his readers with a folksy charm and wit. This persona helped to create a sense of familiarity and trust, making the almanack not just a publication, but a companion that readers turned to year after year. Through Poor Richard, Benjamin was able to address serious topics with a light touch, making his advice both accessible and enjoyable.

The success of *Poor Richard's Almanack* had a significant impact on Benjamin's career and reputation. It established him as a leading figure in colonial American publishing and cemented his reputation as a man of wisdom and humor. The almanack's popularity also provided Benjamin with a steady stream of income, which supported his other ventures and allowed him to pursue his many interests in science, politics, and civic affairs.

In addition to its commercial success, *Poor Richard's Almanack* played a role in shaping American culture and values. Benjamin's aphorisms and practical advice promoted the ideals of hard work, thrift, and self-reliance, which became central to the American way of living. The almanack also encouraged readers to think critically and reflect on their own lives, fostering a culture of self-improvement and personal responsibility.

In the first year of publishing the almanack, Benjamin undertook another pioneering venture by publishing the first German-language newspaper in America, *Die Philadelphische Zeitung*. This endeavor was an indication of Benjamin's recognition of the diverse linguistic and cultural landscape of Pennsylvania, which had a significant population of German-speaking immigrants. Despite his innovative efforts, the newspaper struggled to compete in a rapidly growing market. Within a year, *Die Philadelphische Zeitung* stopped publication, overshadowed by four other newly founded German newspapers that quickly dominated the market.

Benjamin's attempt to establish a German-language newspaper demonstrated his forward-thinking approach and his understanding of the importance of catering to different communities. He recognized the need to provide news and information to the German-speaking population, aiming to integrate them more fully into the fabric of colonial society.

In addition to his work with *Die Philadelphische Zeitung*, Benjamin also contributed to the religious and cultural life of the German-speaking community by printing Moravian religious books in German. The Moravians, a Protestant sect with a strong presence in Pennsylvania, valued their religious texts and needed them in their native language. Benjamin's printing press became an essential resource for producing these religious materials, facilitating the spread of Moravian beliefs and practices among German-speaking settlers.

Benjamin's involvement in printing German-language materials underscored his commitment to supporting the diverse communities of Pennsylvania. By providing German-speaking residents with access to news and religious literature in their language, he helped bridge cultural gaps and promote a sense of inclusion and community cohesion. These efforts, although not always successful in their immediate goals, highlighted Benjamin's broader vision of a connected and informed society, regardless of linguistic and cultural differences.

In all these social and personal happenings, Benjamin was also delving into a newfound interest in playing chess, making him the first chess player known by name in the American colonies. His essay on *The Morals of Chess*, published in the Columbian Magazine in December 1786, is the second known writing on chess in America. This essay, which praised chess and established a code of behavior for the game, has been widely reprinted and translated. Benjamin and a friend used chess as a means of learning the Italian language, assigning tasks such as memorizing parts of Italian grammar to the loser of each game.

Moreover, his social status in Philadelphia kept growing steadily as he expanded his ventures and took on new responsibilities. In 1734, at the age of twenty-eight, Benjamin Franklin was elected Grand Master of the Grand Masonic Lodge of Masons of Pennsylvania, a prestigious and influential position within the Masonic order. The Freemasons were a fraternal organization that emphasized moral development, mutual assistance, and community service among its members. Being elected Grand Master meant that Benjamin was recognized not only for his leadership qualities but also for his integrity, wisdom, and dedication to the values upheld by the Masons.

The role of Grand Master was very important. It involved overseeing the Masonic lodges in the area, making sure they followed the principles and rituals of Freemasonry correctly, and giving advice and guidance to the members. This position solidified Benjamin's standing in the community, as it was a role typically reserved for individuals of high social status and moral character. It connected him with influential figures across the colony, including politicians, businessmen, and other prominent citizens, many of whom were also members of the Masonic order.

Being a Grand Master afforded Benjamin the opportunity to expand his network and influence further. The Masonic Lodge served as a hub for intellectual exchange and social interaction, where members could discuss ideas, share knowledge, and collaborate on various projects. This environment aligned perfectly with Benjamin's interests in self-improvement, civic duty, and community betterment.

Moreover, Benjamin's election as Grand Master reflected his growing reputation and leadership in Philadelphia. It was a testament to the respect and trust he had earned from his peers. The position also allowed him to promote the Masonic values of charity, education, and fraternity, which resonated with his own beliefs and efforts in various civic initiatives.

Around this time, he also began to buy property on Philadelphia's Market Street. Over the years, he strategically acquired several lots, eventually establishing a significant presence that housed his print shop and retail space. This area would later be known as Franklin Court, commemorating his enduring legacy.

Ever resourceful, Benjamin found ways to promote *The Pennsylvania Gazette*, his newspaper. Postmaster Andrew Bradford had forbidden post riders from carrying the Gazette, so Benjamin resorted to bribing the riders to ensure his paper reached its audience. This clever tactic demonstrated his determination to succeed in the competitive world of colonial publishing.

In 1735, Benjamin's brother James passed away, and Benjamin's compassion for his family was evident. He sent James's widow 500 copies of *Poor Richard's Almanack* for free, enabling her to sell them and generate income.

Moreover, in 1735, Andrew Hamilton, a prominent lawyer and supporter of Benjamin Franklin, played a key role in defending John Peter Zenger in a landmark freedom of the press case. This case became a foundational moment in the establishment of press freedom in America and highlighted the interconnected nature of Benjamin's personal and professional networks.

John Peter Zenger was a German immigrant and printer who published the *New York Weekly Journal*. In his newspaper, Zenger openly criticized the corrupt practices of the colonial governor, William Cosby. This criticism led to Zenger's arrest on charges of libel, which, at the time, meant publishing information that opposed the government, regardless of whether the information was true or false.

Zenger's case attracted significant attention and support from those who believed in the importance of a free press. Benjamin Franklin, who was deeply involved in the printing and publishing industry, was among those who recognized the critical implications of Zenger's trial. Benjamin's connection to the case was further strengthened through his relationship with Andrew Hamilton, a highly respected lawyer known for his eloquence and legal acumen.

Hamilton agreed to defend Zenger, despite the risks and challenges involved. His defense strategy was groundbreaking. He argued that Zenger could not be guilty of libel if the statements he published were true, even if they were critical of the government. This was a radical departure from the existing legal standards, which did not consider the truth of the statements as a defense against libel.

During the trial, Hamilton famously addressed the jury, urging them to consider the broader implications of their verdict. He argued that the freedom to criticize government officials was essential to the preservation of liberty and that a free press was a crucial check on power.

The jury was persuaded by Hamilton's arguments and acquitted Zenger, setting a powerful precedent for freedom of the press. This verdict marked a significant victory for the principle that truth should be a defense against libel and underscored the importance of an independent press in safeguarding democracy.

Benjamin's civic engagement deepened in 1736 when he was named Clerk of the Pennsylvania Assembly, a position that allowed him to influence legislative processes. He also began printing currency for New Jersey, showcasing his expanding business operations. However, this year was also marked by tragedy as his young son, Francis Folger, died of smallpox at the age of four. This loss profoundly affected Benjamin and his wife, Deborah.

Undeterred by personal sorrow, Benjamin continued to contribute to the community. He organized the Union Fire Company in 1736, reflecting his commitment to public safety. He remained actively involved in various civic organizations, including the Library Company, the Masonic Lodge, and the Junto, ensuring his presence and influence in Philadelphia's civic life.

Benjamin's printing business continued to thrive, evidenced by his publication of *A Treaty of Friendship held with the Chiefs of the Six Nations at Philadelphia* and the first public use of the Pennsylvania State House, later known as Independence Hall. His efforts in these projects underscored his role in shaping the political and cultural landscape of the colony.

In 1737, Benjamin Franklin's public service career took a significant step forward when he was appointed Postmaster of Philadelphia at the age of thirty-one. He held this position for sixteen long years till 1753. This position provided him with the opportunity to make several important improvements to the postal system, which enhanced communication within the American colonies. Benjamin reorganized the existing mail routes to make them more efficient, introducing new, direct routes that reduced travel time and ensured faster delivery of mail between key cities and towns. This reorganization helped speed up communication, which was crucial for both personal correspondence and the dissemination of news.

Under Benjamin's leadership, the postal system began to offer more regular and reliable mail services. He established a schedule that allowed for consistent and predictable mail delivery, a significant improvement over the irregular service that had previously existed. Benjamin employed post riders who traveled specific routes to deliver and collect mail and set up way stations along these routes where riders could rest and exchange mailbags. These way stations acted as relay points, ensuring that mail could be transported over long distances more quickly and efficiently.

Benjamin also introduced measures to increase postal revenue, such as standardizing postal rates and ensuring that postal workers were paid more consistently. By making the postal system more financially viable, he was able to reinvest in further improvements and expansions. He implemented a system of postal inspections to monitor the performance of post offices and postal workers, ensuring that the standards of service were maintained and that any issues could be quickly identified and addressed.

Utilizing his skills as a printer, Benjamin produced and distributed postal-related materials, such as forms, notices, and advertisements.

This improved the administrative efficiency of the postal service and promoted its use among the public. To deal with undeliverable mail, Benjamin established dead letter offices where undelivered letters and packages were collected and stored. This innovation helped to reduce the loss of mail and allowed senders to retrieve items that could not be delivered.

Benjamin also worked to increase public awareness of the postal service and its benefits. He used his newspaper, *The Pennsylvania Gazette*, to inform the public about new postal routes, services, and changes to the system. This helped to build trust and reliance on the postal service. Benjamin's improvements to the postal system had a lasting impact on communication within the American colonies. His efforts laid the groundwork for a more organized and reliable postal service, which played a crucial role in connecting the colonies and facilitating the exchange of information. This, in turn, contributed to the development of a more cohesive and informed colonial society, helping to pave the way for greater unity and cooperation in the years leading up to the American Revolution.

That same year, the Great Awakening preacher George Whitefield arrived in Philadelphia, drawing enthusiastic crowds. Benjamin Franklin was deeply intrigued by George Whitefield's charisma and printed much of his material, including sermons and pamphlets. Despite their differing religious views, Benjamin admired Whitefield's oratory skills and entrepreneurial spirit.

Whitefield was a prominent preacher during the Great Awakening, a religious revival that swept through the American colonies in the 18th century. His sermons emphasized the need for personal salvation through Jesus Christ and often focused on themes of human sinfulness and divine grace. Whitefield's approach aimed at stirring intense emotional responses from his audience, urging them to experience a personal, transformative relationship with God.

In contrast, Benjamin, influenced by Enlightenment ideals, held more rational and Deistic beliefs. Deism, which was popular among many intellectuals of the time, stated that reason and observation of the natural world, rather than revelation or religious dogma, were the primary sources of knowledge about the universe. Deists typically believed in a Creator who set the universe in motion but did not intervene in human affairs or suspend the natural laws. Consequently, Benjamin's view of religion was more focused on ethics and morality, grounded in rational thought and empirical evidence, rather than emotional religious experiences or the supernatural.

Despite these theological differences, Benjamin and Whitefield maintained a mutually respectful and beneficial relationship. Benjamin appreciated Whitefield's ability to captivate large audiences with his powerful and emotive preaching. He was particularly impressed by Whitefield's talent for fundraising and organizing, qualities that resonated with Benjamin's own entrepreneurial spirit. This admiration led Benjamin to support Whitefield's ministry by printing and distributing his sermons and pamphlets, recognizing the widespread appeal and demand for Whitefield's messages.

Moreover, Benjamin's environmental consciousness was evident in 1739 when he led a protest against the pollution caused by slaughterhouses, tanneries, and other industries near the public docks and streets. This protest highlighted his commitment to public health and the environment, aspects often overlooked in the colonial era.

In 1740, Benjamin's reputation as a printer continued to grow. He became the official printer for New Jersey and printed a vast array of materials for Whitefield, who planned to build a school for African Americans on a 5,000-acre plot (equivalent to approximately 7.81 square miles or 20.23 square kilometers), though the school was never constructed. Benjamin's involvement in these projects demonstrated his support for education and progressive causes.

Benjamin Franklin's early years in Philadelphia marked a period of profound personal and professional growth, characterized by his entrepreneurial spirit, intellectual pursuits, and commitment to community improvement. From the establishment of the Junto and his own print shop to the creation of *Poor Richard's Almanack* and the launch of the first German-language newspaper in America, Benjamin's endeavors showcased his versatility and forward-thinking approach. His relationships with family and friends provided a supportive network that fueled his ambitions, while his innovative contributions to publishing and community projects laid the groundwork for his lasting legacy.

## 3. Pioneering Scientific Exploration

The period from 1741 to 1752 was particularly transformative for Benjamin, as it saw him delve deeply into scientific exploration, contribute to public knowledge, and lay the groundwork for lasting educational institutions.

Continuing from the 1730s and leading into the 1740s, Benjamin documented observations on population growth, noting that the American population was expanding at the fastest rate in the world. He attributed this rapid growth to the plentiful supply of food and the vast availability of farmland in America. Benjamin calculated that the population in America was doubling every twenty years, predicting that it would surpass the population of England within a century.

In 1741, Benjamin Franklin introduced one of his most practical and enduring inventions, the Franklin stove. This innovative heating device was designed to address several inefficiencies and dangers associated with traditional fireplaces. Fireplaces, which were the primary source of heating in colonial American homes, often allowed much of the heat to escape up the chimney, leading to poor heat retention and a significant waste of wood. Additionally, they posed a considerable fire hazard, with open flames and sparks sometimes igniting nearby materials.

Benjamin's design for the stove, also known as the Pennsylvania Fireplace, included a hollow baffle – a metal panel that directed the flow of heat. This genius addition allowed the stove to retain and radiate heat more effectively throughout the room. By controlling the airflow and allowing hot gasses to circulate within the stove before escaping through the chimney, the Franklin stove maximized the heat output from a smaller amount of wood. This not only made homes warmer and more comfortable but also provided a cost-effective and resource-efficient solution to heating.

The stove's design significantly reduced the amount of wood needed for heating, which was particularly beneficial at a time when wood was a valuable and sometimes scarce resource. Benjamin's stove also minimized the risk of chimney fires, a common and dangerous problem with open hearths. By containing the fire within a closed structure and controlling the exhaust of hot gasses, the stove made heating safer for households.

Benjamin's innovation in heating technology was an example of his ability to apply scientific principles to solve practical problems. He was deeply interested in understanding the mechanics of heat transfer and the behavior of gasses. Through careful observation and experimentation, he developed a solution that improved everyday life, demonstrating his commitment to the Enlightenment ideals of reason, science, and progress.

Around the same time, Benjamin also ventured into publishing with *The General Magazine and Historical Chronicle*, one of America's earliest magazines. Despite its initial promise, the magazine failed after just six issues. This setback did not deter Benjamin; instead, it fueled his determination to continue exploring and sharing knowledge through different mediums.

In 1742, Benjamin turned his attention to the natural sciences. He organized and publicized a project to sponsor plant-collecting trips by John Bartram, a renowned Philadelphia botanist. Benjamin recognized the importance of Bartram's work in cataloging North American flora and saw it as a means to contribute to the global scientific community. This initiative highlighted Benjamin's belief in the value of collaborative scientific endeavors and his commitment to advancing knowledge.

Benjamin's interest in science deepened further in 1743 when he attended Archibald Spencer's lectures on natural philosophy in Boston. Spencer was a well-regarded lecturer whose presentations on various scientific topics were gaining popularity in the colonies. Overall, these lectures delved into subjects such as electricity, magnetism, and other natural phenomena, providing a comprehensive overview of the emerging scientific understanding of the time. Benjamin, already an avid reader and self-taught scholar, found himself captivated by Spencer's detailed explanations and demonstrations.

The exposure to these lectures profoundly impacted Benjamin, igniting a fascination with the natural world and the underlying principles that governed it. He was particularly intrigued by the mysteries of electricity, a relatively new and poorly understood field. Spencer used static electricity in his demonstrations, captivating Benjamin with the mysterious and intriguing nature of this invisible force. Static electricity refers to the accumulation of electric charge on the surface of objects, which remains in place until discharged. In his experiments, Spencer would create static electricity by rubbing materials together, a process known as triboelectric charging. This simple yet powerful demonstration sparked Benjamin's curiosity and set him on a path of scientific investigation.

Benjamin proposed a revolutionary idea that "vitreous" and "resinous" electricity were not different types of "electrical fluid," as was commonly believed at the time. Instead, he suggested that they were the same "fluid" under different pressures. To understand this, it's important to know that in the 18th century, electricity was thought of as a fluid that could flow from one object to another. "Vitreous electricity" was associated with glass-like materials, while "resinous electricity" was associated with resin-like materials. Benjamin's insight was that these two forms of electricity were not fundamentally different but represented the same phenomenon manifesting under different conditions.

Interestingly, William Watson, a British scientist, independently arrived at the same conclusion that year, demonstrating the parallel advancements in electrical theory on both sides of the Atlantic Ocean.

Benjamin's most significant contribution to the study of electricity was his introduction of the terms "positive" and "negative" charges. Before this, scientists referred to electrical charges as "vitreous" (positive) and "resinous" (negative), based on the materials that produced them. Benjamin's new terminology simplified the understanding of electrical interactions. He used the terms "positive" and "negative" to describe the relative abundance or deficiency of electrical fluid. This was a groundbreaking simplification that made the study of electricity more accessible and easier to understand.

Moreover, Benjamin was the pioneer in discovering the principle of conservation of charge. This principle states that the total amount of electric charge in an isolated system remains constant, regardless of any changes that take place within the system. In other words, charge can neither be created nor destroyed, only transferred from one part of the system to another. This discovery was crucial because it provided a foundational law for the study of electricity, akin to the conservation laws in mechanics and thermodynamics.

Moreover, inspired by the ideas and knowledge he gained from Spencer's lectures, Benjamin decided to take action to promote scientific inquiry and intellectual exchange in the American colonies. He published *A Proposal for Promoting Useful Knowledge*, a visionary document outlining his ideas for fostering a community of scholars and scientists dedicated to the pursuit of knowledge and the betterment of society. This proposal called for the formation of a society where individuals could come together to share discoveries, discuss scientific advancements, and collaborate on research projects.

Benjamin's proposal led to the founding of the American Philosophical Society in 1744. The society's mission was to gather like-minded individuals who shared Benjamin's passion for science and intellectual exploration. It aimed to create a forum where members could engage in discussions, present their findings, and inspire one another to further the collective understanding of the natural world.

The American Philosophical Society quickly became a focal point for scientific activity in the colonies. Its meetings attracted a diverse group of thinkers, including scientists, philosophers, and inventors, who were eager to contribute to the society's goals. The society's members conducted experiments, exchanged ideas through correspondence, and published their findings in scientific journals. This collaborative environment fostered a spirit of innovation and intellectual rigor that significantly advanced the scientific community in America.

One of the society's earliest projects was the sponsorship of John Bartram's botanical expeditions. Benjamin recognized the importance of cataloging and studying the diverse plant life in North America. By supporting Bartram's efforts, the society contributed valuable knowledge to the global scientific community and demonstrated its commitment to promoting useful knowledge.

The society also played a crucial role in connecting American scientists with their European counterparts. Benjamin's extensive correspondence with prominent scientists like Peter Collinson in London facilitated the exchange of ideas and findings across the Atlantic. This transatlantic dialogue enriched the society's knowledge base and positioned American scientists as active contributors to the global scientific community.

The founding of the American Philosophical Society marked a significant milestone in Benjamin's scientific journey. It embodied his belief in the power of collective inquiry and the importance of sharing knowledge for the common good. The society's establishment provided a structured and supportive environment for scientific exploration, enabling Benjamin and his peers to pursue their intellectual passions and make substantial contributions to the advancement of science.

The same year marked a joyous occasion in Benjamin's personal life with the birth of his daughter, Sarah, affectionately known as Sally. She was baptized at Christ Church in Philadelphia, further rooting Benjamin in the community he served.

Tragedy struck in 1745 with the death of Benjamin's father, Josiah. This loss was a profound moment for Benjamin, as Josiah had been a guiding influence in his life, instilling in him the values of hard work, education, and perseverance. Despite the personal grief, Benjamin's resolve to contribute to society remained undiminished.

In 1747, Benjamin Franklin actively engaged in public affairs by publishing *The Plain Truth*, a compelling pamphlet that argued for better military preparedness in Pennsylvania. At that time, the colony faced numerous external threats, including potential attacks from French forces and their Native American allies. Pennsylvania's lack of a formal militia\* and adequate defenses left it vulnerable, prompting Benjamin to take action.

*The Plain Truth* was more than just a call to arms; it was a well-reasoned argument that underscored the necessity of unity and collective action for the colony's security. Benjamin articulated the dangers that Pennsylvania faced and emphasized the need for organized defense measures to protect the settlers and their

---

\* A militia is a military force composed of ordinary citizens rather than professional soldiers. These citizens are trained to serve as soldiers in times of emergency or conflict. Militias are typically used for local defense and security and can be called upon to supplement regular armed forces during times of war or crisis. Historically, militias have been essential in various countries for providing rapid and flexible responses to threats when a standing army is not available or sufficient. Members of a militia usually have civilian jobs and lives but undergo periodic training to maintain their readiness to serve when needed.

properties. He urged the citizens to recognize the gravity of the situation and to support the establishment of a militia.

One of the most notable features of *The Plain Truth* was the inclusion of the first political cartoon published in America. This cartoon, famously depicting a snake divided into eight segments, each representing a different American colony, carried the caption "Join, or Die." The imagery of the disunited snake symbolized the fragmented and ineffective state of the colonies' defense efforts. Benjamin's message was clear: only through unity could the colonies hope to defend themselves against common enemies.

The "Join, or Die" cartoon was a powerful visual representation of Benjamin's call for colonial unity and cooperation. At a time when the American colonies operated largely independently of one another, the cartoon underscored the idea that their survival depended on working together. It was a stark reminder that division and disunity would lead to their collective downfall, whereas unity would ensure their strength and resilience.

Benjamin's pamphlet and the accompanying cartoon had a significant impact. They spurred discussions about the need for a coordinated defense strategy and helped to galvanize public support for the formation of a militia. Benjamin's persuasive writing and the striking visual aid of the political cartoon effectively communicated the urgency of the situation and the importance of unity in the face of external threats.

Despite his growing involvement in public matters, Benjamin continued his scientific pursuits. In 1748, he joined the Pennsylvania militia, declining a commission as a colonel due to his lack of military experience. This period also saw Benjamin's contributions to education. In 1749, he presented his vision for a new educational institution in a pamphlet titled *Publick Academy of Philadelphia*. This vision ultimately led to the founding of the University of Pennsylvania, an institution that emphasized practical education alongside classical studies.

Benjamin's scientific achievements began to gain recognition beyond American shores. In 1751, Peter Collinson published Benjamin's letters on electricity in London, bringing his groundbreaking research to a wider audience. These letters documented Benjamin's experiments and theories, solidifying his reputation as a leading scientist of his time.

The pinnacle of Benjamin Franklin's electrical research came in 1752 with his famous kite experiment, a groundbreaking endeavor that forever changed the understanding of electricity. Determined to prove his theory that lightning was a form of electricity, Benjamin devised an experiment that involved flying a kite during a thunderstorm – a daring and dangerous undertaking.

Benjamin constructed a simple kite using a silk handkerchief stretched over a wooden frame. He attached a metal wire to the top of the kite and secured it with a length of hemp string, which was a good conductor of electricity. At the end of the string, he tied a silk ribbon and a key, the silk providing insulation to protect him from electrical shocks.

On a stormy day in June 1752, Benjamin and his son William, who assisted him, ventured out to an open field. They launched the kite into the stormy sky and waited. As the kite ascended and was struck by lightning, Benjamin observed that the loose fibers of the hemp string stood erect, indicating the presence of electrical charge. He then moved his hand close to the key and felt a spark, confirming his hypothesis that lightning was indeed electrical in nature.

This experiment not only proved that lightning was a form of electricity but also demonstrated that the atmosphere could carry an electrical charge. Benjamin's findings were revolutionary, as they provided the first direct evidence of the electrical nature of lightning, bridging the gap between everyday electrical phenomena and the powerful forces of nature.

The success of the kite experiment led to the invention of the lightning rod, a practical application of Benjamin's discoveries. He designed the lightning rod to protect buildings from lightning strikes by providing a controlled path for the electrical charge to travel safely to the ground. The device consisted of a pointed metal rod mounted on the highest part of a building, connected to the ground by a conductor. This invention significantly reduced the risk of fire and structural damage caused by lightning, making it a vital safety feature for buildings.

Benjamin's lightning rod was quickly adopted in America and Europe, significantly improving public safety and demonstrating the practical benefits of scientific research. His invention marked a major advancement in the field of electrical engineering and showcased his ability to apply scientific principles to solve real-world problems.

For his groundbreaking contributions to the study of electricity, Benjamin received the prestigious Copley Medal from the Royal Society of London in 1753. The Copley Medal, one of the highest honors in science, recognized Benjamin's experimental ingenuity and the profound impact of his discoveries. This accolade not only celebrated Benjamin's achievements but also cemented his reputation as a leading scientist of his time.

Benjamin's work on electricity extended beyond the kite experiment and the invention of the lightning rod. He introduced several key concepts that remain fundamental to the study of electricity today, such as the idea of positive and negative charges, the conservation of charge, and the understanding of electrical conductors and insulators. His methodical approach to experimentation and his clear, communicative style in writing about his findings helped disseminate his ideas widely, influencing contemporaries and future generations of scientists.

In the same year, Benjamin's influence in colonial affairs grew with his appointment as Deputy Postmaster General of North America. This position allowed him to even further improve the postal system, enhancing communication across the colonies. Benjamin also wrote a plan for a union of the colonies for security and defense, an early precursor to the ideas that would later shape the United States.

Throughout these years, Benjamin's diverse interests and talents flourished. His scientific experiments, public service, and educational initiatives were all driven by a profound curiosity and a desire to apply knowledge for the betterment of society. His ability to seamlessly integrate his personal, professional, and scientific pursuits made him a true Renaissance man, leaving an unremovable mark on American history.

The period from 1741 to 1752 was a time of remarkable growth and achievement for Benjamin Franklin. His contributions to science, education, and public service were driven by a relentless pursuit of knowledge and a desire to apply that knowledge for the greater good. Benjamin's legacy during these years is a testament to the power of curiosity, innovation, and civic responsibility, principles that continue to inspire future generations. His life during this period was a mosaic of intellectual curiosity, practical invention, and dedicated public service, encapsulating the spirit of the Enlightenment and laying the groundwork for his enduring influence on American society.

## 4. Advocate for Unity and Education

In 1754, as tensions between the British colonies and French forces in North America intensified, Benjamin Franklin stepped forward with a bold and visionary proposal at the Albany Congress. Assembled to address the impending threat of French invasion and to foster greater cooperation among the colonies, the Albany Congress was a critical meeting of colonial representatives. Benjamin, always the forward thinker, saw an opportunity not only to address the immediate military concerns but also to lay the groundwork for a more unified and cooperative colonial governance structure.

Benjamin presented what would become known as the Albany Plan of Union, an ambitious proposal aimed at creating a centralized government for the Thirteen Colonies. This proposed government would have the authority to charge taxes, raise armies, and regulate Indian affairs. The plan envisioned a Grand Council composed of representatives from each colony, presided over by a President-General appointed by the British Crown. This council would have powers to make laws, charge taxes for defense, and manage relations with Native American tribes, which were crucial in the context of the French and Indian War.

The Albany Plan of Union was revolutionary in its scope and foresight. It was the first significant proposal to conceive of the colonies as a collective entity rather than separate, autonomous provinces. Benjamin's plan was a reflection of his belief in the necessity of unity for the common defense and the overall prosperity of the colonies. He understood that fragmented efforts would be insufficient to counter the well-coordinated French military operations and their alliances with various Native American tribes.

Although the plan was ultimately rejected by both the colonial assemblies and the British Crown, the reasons for its rejection were varied. Many colonial assemblies were reluctant to relinquish any degree of their autonomy or tax-levying powers to a central authority. They feared that such a union could undermine their local control and fiscal independence. On the other hand, the British Crown viewed the plan with suspicion, concerned that a unified colonial government might become too powerful and difficult to control, potentially sowing the seeds of independence.

Despite its rejection, the Albany Plan of Union laid the foundational groundwork for future discussions on colonial unity and governance. It was a precursor to the Articles of Confederation and, eventually, the United States Constitution. Benjamin's foresight in proposing such a union highlighted his visionary approach to colonial cooperation and self-governance. He recognized that the colonies' strength lay in their unity, a principle that would become increasingly evident as the struggle for independence unfolded.

The Albany Plan of Union was more than just a proposal for immediate military coordination; it was a blueprint for a new kind of political structure in North America. It demonstrated Benjamin's ability to think beyond the present challenges and envision a future where the colonies could act collectively for their mutual benefit. His plan included provisions for shared financial responsibility, collective security, and a unified approach to diplomacy with Native American tribes, all of which were crucial elements in the emerging concept of a united colonial front.

Benjamin's relentless pursuit of a unified colonial government did not end with the Albany Congress. He continued to advocate for greater cooperation and unity among the colonies in various capacities, whether through his writings, diplomatic efforts, or participation in subsequent congresses and conventions. His work during this period set the stage for the development of the Articles of Confederation, which provided a loose framework for governance during the early years of the American Revolution, and later the United States Constitution, which established a more robust federal structure.

Between 1757 and 1762, Benjamin Franklin resided in England as an agent for the Pennsylvania Assembly, and later extended his representation to include Massachusetts, Georgia, and New Jersey. His primary mission during this period was to advocate for colonial interests, particularly concerning the controversial issues surrounding the proprietors* of Pennsylvania. The proprietors, who held significant political power and land rights, often clashed with the elected colonial assembly over governance and financial matters. Benjamin's role was to present the grievances of the Pennsylvania Assembly to the British government and seek redress for what the colonists viewed as unfair proprietary practices.

Benjamin's diplomatic skills and persuasive arguments quickly made him an effective representative. He was known for his ability to communicate complex issues in a clear and compelling manner, which earned him respect and influence in British political circles.

---

* Proprietors in the context of colonial America refers to individuals or groups who were granted ownership and governing rights over large tracts of land by the British Crown. These proprietors had significant control over the colonies' land distribution, governance, and economic activities. They could sell or lease land, establish towns, and impose taxes and laws.

His charm, wit, and rational approach allowed him to build strong relationships with key figures, including members of Parliament and other influential policymakers. Benjamin's presence in England also gave him the opportunity to engage with prominent intellectuals and scientists of the Enlightenment, furthering his reputation as a leading thinker of his time.

During his stay in England, Benjamin was involved in various important negotiations and discussions. One of his significant achievements was his work on the Penn family's charter, which sought to address the imbalance of power between the proprietors and the colonial assembly. Benjamin's efforts contributed to a broader understanding and eventual reforms in the governance of Pennsylvania, highlighting his effectiveness as a mediator and advocate for colonial rights.

In addition to his political and diplomatic activities, Benjamin actively engaged in scientific and intellectual discussions. He frequented the Royal Society and other scholarly gatherings, where he exchanged ideas with some of the most brilliant minds of the era. These interactions enriched his own scientific pursuits and allowed him to contribute to the broader Enlightenment discourse. Benjamin's involvement in these circles further solidified his status as an eminent figure in both the American and European intellectual communities.

In 1759, Benjamin's contributions to science, public administration, and diplomacy were formally recognized when he was awarded an honorary degree of Doctor of Laws from the University of St. Andrews in Scotland. This prestigious honor was a testament to his multifaceted achievements and his impact on various fields. The degree acknowledged not only his scientific innovations, such as his experiments with electricity and the invention of the lightning rod, but also his efforts in improving public services, such as the postal system, and his diplomatic endeavors on behalf of the American colonies.

The honorary degree from St. Andrews was particularly significant because it was one of the oldest and most respected institutions of higher learning in Europe. The recognition from such a venerable university underscored the broad impact of Benjamin's work and his international stature as a leading intellectual and public servant. This accolade also helped to elevate the status of American intellectual contributions in the eyes of the European elite, paving the way for greater transatlantic collaboration and respect.

Benjamin's time in England was marked by his relentless pursuit of knowledge and his dedication to advocating for colonial interests. He balanced his diplomatic responsibilities with his scientific curiosities, embodying the ideals of the Enlightenment. His ability to navigate the political landscape of the British Empire while maintaining his commitment to the welfare of the American colonies highlighted his exceptional skills as a statesman and a thinker.

During these years as a civil servant and diplomat in England, where chess was more popular than in America, Benjamin also had the opportunity to play against stronger opposition, improving his skills by facing more experienced players. He regularly attended Old Slaughter's Coffee House in London for chess and socializing, making many important personal contacts.

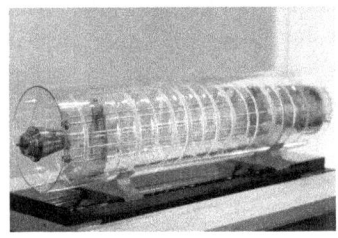

Upon returning to America in 1762, Benjamin mapped postal routes in the colonies, continuing his efforts to improve the postal system. His meticulous mapping ensured more efficient and reliable mail delivery, which was crucial for communication and commerce. In the same year, he invented the glass armonica, a musical instrument that produced ethereal sounds by using a series of glass bowls or goblets of different sizes. The armonica gained popularity in Europe and America, with notable composers like Mozart and Beethoven writing music for it.

Benjamin's scientific aspirations continued with his charting of the Gulf Stream in 1764-65. By documenting the warm Atlantic Ocean current, Benjamin provided valuable information for sailors, significantly reducing travel time between Europe and America. His observations on the Gulf Stream were a critical contribution to oceanography and navigational science.

In 1766, Benjamin Franklin was summoned to testify before the British House of Commons, a pivotal moment in the escalating conflict between the American colonies and Britain. The issue at hand was the Stamp Act, a deeply unpopular piece of legislation that imposed direct taxes on a wide variety of printed materials in the colonies, including newspapers, legal documents, and licenses. This act was part of Britain's attempt to raise revenue from the colonies following the costly Seven Years' War, but it was met with widespread resistance and protest from the colonists, who argued that it violated their rights as Englishmen to be taxed without their consent.

Benjamin's testimony before the House of Commons was a masterclass in diplomacy and persuasive argumentation. He presented the colonists' grievances clearly and compellingly, emphasizing that the Stamp Act was not only economically burdensome but also politically untenable. Benjamin articulated the principle of "no taxation without representation," highlighting the colonists' belief that they should not be subject to taxes imposed by a Parliament in which they had no elected representatives. His reasoned arguments underscored the injustice of the Act and its potential to inflame colonial unrest.

Benjamin's fluency in arguments and deep understanding of colonial affairs made a significant impact on the members of Parliament. He cleverly navigated the complexities of British politics, addressing concerns and countering objections with poise and intelligence. His performance during the testimony played a crucial role in persuading Parliament to repeal the Stamp Act in March 1766, a decision that temporarily alleviated some of the tensions between Britain and the colonies and was celebrated as a major victory in America.

The success of Benjamin's testimony solidified his reputation as a leading advocate for colonial rights and a skilled diplomat. In recognition of his contributions to the colonial cause and his growing influence, he was appointed as the Colonial Agent for

Georgia in 1768, New Jersey in 1769, and Massachusetts in 1770. These appointments were a testament to the trust and respect he commanded among the colonial assemblies, who relied on his ability to represent their interests effectively before the British government.

As a Colonial Agent, Benjamin's responsibilities were multidimensional. He acted as the liaison* between the colonial governments and the British authorities, conveying the colonies' concerns, negotiating on their behalf, and seeking to influence British policies in ways that would benefit the colonies. Benjamin's deep knowledge of both colonial and British political landscapes made him uniquely suited for this role. He was adept at articulating the colonies' positions and advocating for their rights, whether it involved disputes over land claims, trade regulations, or the broader issue of colonial autonomy.

Benjamin's role as a Colonial Agent also involved addressing specific grievances and working to resolve conflicts that arose between the colonies and the British administration. For instance, he was instrumental in addressing issues related to the implementation of the Townshend Acts, another series of taxes imposed on the colonies that provoked further unrest. Benjamin's diplomatic efforts aimed to mitigate the impact of these taxes and to argue for their repeal, continuing his mission to protect colonial interests.

Throughout his tenure as a Colonial Agent, Benjamin maintained an active engagement with both political and intellectual circles in Britain. He used his extensive network of contacts, including influential politicians, intellectuals, and fellow scientists, to build support for the colonial cause. Benjamin's ability to move seamlessly between different spheres of influence underscored his versatility and his effectiveness as a statesman.

In addition to his political and diplomatic activities, Benjamin

---

\* Liaison refers to a person or entity that facilitates communication and cooperation between groups or individuals to ensure effective collaboration and mutual understanding. It can also refer to the act of establishing and maintaining these connections. In a broader sense, a liaison helps coordinate activities, share information, and resolve issues among different parties.

continued to pursue his scientific interests while in Britain. He maintained correspondence with prominent scientists and philosophers, contributing to the vibrant intellectual community of the Enlightenment. His scientific reputation further enhanced his credibility and influence, enabling him to engage with a broad range of issues from a position of respect and authority.

During his time in England, Benjamin also continued to engage with leading scientists like Joseph Priestley, David Hume, and Sir John Pringle, facilitating the dissemination of Enlightenment ideals and scientific knowledge. Benjamin's  interactions with these luminaries enriched his own understanding and reinforced his role as a bridge between the Old World and the New.

In addition to his diplomatic and scientific endeavors, Benjamin remained deeply involved in various civic and community projects. His founding of the Philadelphia Contributionship for Insuring of Houses from Loss by Fire exemplified his commitment to practical philanthropy and public service. This organization not only provided financial protection against fire damage but also promoted fire safety measures, reducing the risk of catastrophic losses for homeowners.

Throughout these years, Benjamin's ability to balance his roles as a scientist, inventor, diplomat, and public servant was truly remarkable. His diverse contributions helped shape the emerging American society, laying the groundwork for future advancements in various fields.

Benjamin's ability to navigate the political landscape of the British Empire, while maintaining his commitment to the welfare of the American colonies, solidified his reputation as a leading statesman and thinker. His honorary degrees from prestigious institutions like Harvard, Yale, and the University of St. Andrews reflected the widespread recognition of his contributions to science, education, and public life.

## We're half way there: A note from Scott Matthews

As we reach the midpoint of this book, exploring the extraordinary life of Benjamin Franklin, I want to extend my heartfelt thanks to you. Writing this narrative has been a labor of love, driven by deep admiration for Benjamin's brilliance and a desire to share his story with you.

Your insights and feedback are incredibly valuable, not only to me but also to others who seek to understand the importance of Benjamin's legacy. Your reviews help support my work as a storyteller and contribute to the broader appreciation of Benjamin's achievements in science, politics, and culture. I genuinely appreciate every review, cherishing your thoughts and suggestions for further exploration.

If you have been inspired by the pages so far or have ideas on how we can continue Benjamin's journey together, I encourage you to share your thoughts. A QR code is provided below for your convenience, directing you to Amazon where you can leave your review. Whether you're reading a digital or physical copy, a quick scan or click allows you to share your reflections.

Thank you for being part of this journey. Your feedback not only shapes the narrative but also honors Benjamin Franklin's enduring spirit. Here's to the upcoming chapters and the valuable lessons they hold.

## 5. Diplomatic Endeavors and Political Strides

From 1771 to 1781, Benjamin Franklin navigated a period of extraordinary personal and political upheaval, solidifying his legacy as one of the most influential figures in American history. This decade saw Benjamin embark on international diplomatic missions, engage in pivotal political maneuvers, and experience profound personal losses.

In 1771, Benjamin Franklin embarked on a tour of Ireland, a journey that offered him a firsthand view of the political and social conditions in another British-controlled territory. Benjamin's travels through Ireland were marked by his keen observations and reflections on the similarities and differences between the Irish and American colonies. This journey was more than merely a leisurely trip. It also provided a crucial educational experience that deepened his understanding of the broader implications of British colonial rule.

During his tour, Benjamin visited several key cities and regions, including Dublin, Belfast, and the rural countryside. In Dublin, he observed the stark contrast between the opulence of the British aristocracy and the abject poverty of the local Irish population. The city's grandeur, with its grand estates and well-maintained public buildings, stood in sharp contrast to the squalor in which many of the Irish lived. Benjamin was particularly struck by the visible signs of economic disparity and the impact of British policies on the Irish people's quality of life.

Benjamin's interactions with the local Irish people provided him with valuable insights into their daily struggles. He listened to stories of heavy taxation, restrictive trade practices, and the suppression of Irish cultural and religious practices. These conversations highlighted the widespread discontent and resentment toward British rule, which resonated deeply with Benjamin. He saw parallels between the Irish grievances and those of the American colonists, particularly regarding issues of taxation without representation and the lack of political autonomy.

One notable aspect of Benjamin's trip was his meeting with prominent Irish leaders and intellectuals. He engaged in discussions with figures such as Henry Grattan, a leading advocate for Irish legislative independence, and Edmund Burke, an influential statesman and philosopher who would later become a vocal critic of British policy in America. These exchanges were intellectually stimulating for Benjamin and reinforced his belief in the universal struggle for self-determination and governance free from oppressive control.

In Belfast, Benjamin was impressed by the spirit of industry and resilience among the Irish Protestants, who were economically and politically marginalized despite their significant contributions to the local economy. He observed their determination to improve their circumstances through hard work and community solidarity. This spirit of resilience reminded Benjamin of the enterprising spirit of the American colonists and their potential to thrive if given the freedom to govern themselves.

As Benjamin traveled through the Irish countryside, he witnessed the dire effects of agricultural policies imposed by the British, which prioritized the interests of English landowners over the welfare of Irish tenants. The sight of impoverished farmers struggling to eke out a living on meager plots of land left a profound impression on Benjamin. He understood that the economic exploitation and lack of political representation experienced by the Irish were mirrored in the American colonies.

Benjamin's observations in Ireland were not limited to economic and political issues; he also took note of the social and cultural dimensions of British rule. He saw how British policies aimed to suppress the Irish language, traditions, and Catholic faith, much like the efforts to undermine local customs and governance in America. This cultural suppression was yet another parallel that underscored the broader theme of colonial subjugation.

This trip further solidified Benjamin's understanding of colonial struggles and injustices, reinforcing his commitment to advocating for American independence. The parallels he drew between the Irish experience and the situation in the American colonies convinced him that the quest for freedom and self-governance was not only just but necessary. He returned to America with a renewed sense of purpose, determined to work toward a future where the colonies could break free from British tyranny and establish a government that truly represented the people.

Alongside his trip to Ireland, between 1771 and 1772, Benjamin Franklin began writing his autobiography, a project that would span several years and become one of his most enduring and influential works. Initially intended as a private memoir for his son, William, the autobiography evolved into a comprehensive account of Benjamin's life, filled with reflections, advice, and anecdotes that provide a window into his early life, career, and the values that shaped his character.

The year 1774 brought significant challenges for Benjamin Franklin, thrusting him into the heart of a major political scandal known as the "Hutchinson Affair." This controversy erupted when private letters written by Thomas Hutchinson, the Royal Governor of Massachusetts, were leaked and published in America. Hutchinson's letters, addressed to British officials, contained candid remarks advocating for more repressive measures to control the increasingly restless American colonists. The revelation of these letters confirmed the colonists' worst fears about the intentions of their British rulers, fueling the flames of discontent and rebellion.

Benjamin played a pivotal role in this scandal. As the colonial agent in London, he had come into possession of Hutchinson's letters, which were initially intended to remain confidential. Recognizing their explosive content, Benjamin believed that making these letters public would expose the true nature of British colonial policies and increase support for the colonial cause. He sent copies of the letters to friends in Massachusetts, who then arranged for their publication in local newspapers. The reaction was swift and furious. The colonists were outraged by Hutchinson's betrayal, and the letters became a rallying point for those advocating resistance to British rule.

The British government responded with equal intensity. In January 1774, Benjamin was summoned before the Privy Council in London to account for his role in the leak. The hearing, held in the Cockpit, a room in the Palace of Whitehall, quickly devolved into a brutal character assassination orchestrated by Solicitor General Alexander Wedderburn. Wedderburn seized the opportunity to publicly humiliate Benjamin, accusing him of theft and treason. He depicted Benjamin as a deceitful and disloyal opportunist, seeking to undermine the British government for personal gain.

Wedderburn's scathing attack was intended not only to discredit Benjamin but also to send a clear message to other colonial agents and sympathizers. The spectacle was designed to reinforce British authority and intimidate those who might support the growing resistance in the colonies. Benjamin stood stoically through the tirade, absorbing the verbal onslaught with remarkable composure.

Despite the personal and professional humiliation, he understood the broader implications of the event.

The Privy Council's harsh treatment of Benjamin did not have the intended effect of diminishing colonial hatred. Instead, it further exposed the British government's contempt for colonial rights and deepened the resolve of those advocating for American independence. Benjamin's dignified silence in the face of Wedderburn's abuse resonated with many, highlighting his commitment to the colonial cause and his willingness to endure personal sacrifice for the greater good.

In the aftermath of the Privy Council hearing, Benjamin's reputation in Britain was severely damaged, but his stature in America was significantly enhanced. He became a symbol of colonial resistance, embodying the struggle for justice and self-determination. The Hutchinson Affair, and Benjamin's role in it, underscored the deepening divide between the colonies and the British government, making reconciliation increasingly unlikely.

Despite the intense pressure and the personal cost, Benjamin remained steadfast in his resolve. He continued to advocate for colonial rights and to seek peaceful solutions to the escalating conflict. However, the events of 1774 marked a turning point in his thinking. He began to see more clearly that the British government was unlikely to make the concessions necessary for a fair and just resolution. This realization pushed Benjamin closer to the cause of independence.

Benjamin's experience with the Hutchinson Affair also influenced his diplomatic strategies. He recognized the importance of international support for the colonial cause and began to consider more seriously the potential for alliances with foreign powers. His subsequent diplomatic mission to France, where he successfully secured French support for the American Revolution, was informed by the lessons he had learned from his time in London.

Tragedy struck Benjamin Franklin's personal life later in 1774 when his beloved wife of forty-four years, Deborah Read, passed away in Philadelphia at the age of sixty-six. Deborah's death was a profound loss for Benjamin, marking the end of a partnership that had been a cornerstone of his personal and professional life. Despite the long periods of separation due to Benjamin's work in England and his various diplomatic missions, their marriage had been a source of unwavering strength and stability for him.

Throughout their marriage, Deborah had proved to be a steadfast and competent partner. She managed their household and business affairs with remarkable skill, overseeing the day-to-day operations of Benjamin's printing business and later their general store. Her practical intelligence and strong will allowed Benjamin the freedom to pursue his numerous scientific experiments, public service, and political endeavors without worrying about the home front.

Deborah's role extended beyond mere management; she was a critical pillar in Benjamin's life, providing emotional support and practical advice. Her understanding of business and her ability to handle financial matters ensured the family's prosperity during Benjamin's frequent absences.

Deborah's health had been declining for several years before her death. She suffered a series of strokes, the first of which occurred in 1768, which left her partially paralyzed. Despite her condition, she continued to manage their affairs to the best of her ability. Her resilience and determination were evident even as her health continued to deteriorate. In Benjamin's letters, he often expressed concern for her well-being and his frustration at being unable to be by her side during her illness.

Deborah's death in December 1774 left a significant void in Benjamin's life. He received the news while he was in England, dealing with the aftermath of the Hutchinson Affair and advocating for colonial rights. The distance made the loss even more extreme, as Benjamin was unable to be with Deborah in her final moments or to attend her funeral. Her passing marked the end of a partnership that had profoundly shaped his life and career.

Despite his immense grief, Benjamin continued to press on with his public duties, driven by a deep sense of responsibility to his country and its cause. He channeled his sorrow into his work, recognizing that the fight for American independence required his full attention and effort. The loss of Deborah, however, was a constant source of sadness for Benjamin. In his letters and writings, he occasionally reflected on their life together and the profound impact she had on him.

Deborah's legacy lived on through Benjamin's continued achievements and their daughter Sarah, known as Sally, who provided him with emotional support in the years following her mother's death. Sally, along with her own children, became a source of comfort for Benjamin, who cherished his family connections deeply, especially in the absence of his beloved Deborah. This familial support was crucial as Benjamin faced one of the most tumultuous periods of his life, both personally and politically.

In 1775, not long after Deborah's passing, Benjamin was elected as a delegate from Pennsylvania to the Second Continental Congress, a pivotal assembly that would steer the American colonies toward independence. This appointment came at a critical juncture, as tensions between the colonies and Britain were escalating rapidly. Benjamin's profound grief over Deborah's death did not deter him from his duties; rather, it seemed to reinforce his resolve to fight for the principles of liberty and justice that he and Deborah had long valued.

During this time, Benjamin also served as chairman of the Pennsylvania Committee of Safety, responsible for coordinating the colony's defenses. His leadership and experience were invaluable as the colonies prepared for the impending conflict with Britain. Benjamin's strategic thinking and diplomatic skills were crucial in unifying the disparate colonies and rallying them to the cause of independence. He recognized that the success of the revolutionary movement depended on effective organization and communication, both areas in which he excelled.

One of Benjamin's significant contributions in 1775 was his appointment as Postmaster General of the Colonies. This role leveraged his extensive experience in improving postal services, a field he had revolutionized decades earlier. Benjamin understood that a reliable communication network was essential for coordinating the revolutionary efforts across the vast and geographically dispersed colonies. His reforms in the postal system enhanced the flow of information and facilitated the effective dissemination of revolutionary ideas and strategies. Under his leadership, the postal system became a vital tool in the coordination and mobilization of the colonial resistance.

Benjamin's dual roles in the Second Continental Congress and as Postmaster General demonstrated his many-sided talents and his unwavering dedication to the American cause. He worked tirelessly to ensure that the colonies were united in their efforts against Britain. His ability to see the bigger picture and to strategize accordingly helped to lay the groundwork for the eventual success of the American Revolution.

The same year, Benjamin was also involved in diplomatic efforts to secure foreign support for the American cause. He understood that the newly idealized nation would need allies to sustain its fight for independence. His reputation as a statesman and scientist had already garnered him respect on the international stage, making him an ideal candidate to represent American interests abroad.

As the conflict with Britain intensified, Benjamin's leadership and vision became even more critical. His ability to inspire and mobilize others was evident in his efforts to prepare the colonies for war. He was instrumental in organizing the militia and ensuring that the colonies had the necessary resources to sustain the fight. His work with the Committee of Safety included overseeing the production and distribution of arms and ammunition, as well as implementing measures to protect key infrastructure from British attacks.

Benjamin's personal resilience during this period was remarkable. Despite the profound loss of Deborah, he continued to serve his country with unwavering dedication. Sally's support and the comfort of his grandchildren provided him with the emotional strength needed to persevere. The bond between Benjamin and Sally was strengthened by their shared commitment to the cause of independence and their mutual support during a time of great uncertainty and danger.

In 1776, Benjamin Franklin played a central role in shaping the future of Pennsylvania and the emerging nation through a series of pivotal actions and decisions. His influence extended from the state level to the international stage, demonstrating his talents as a leader, diplomat, and advocate for independence.

Benjamin's first major contribution that year was his role in presiding over the Pennsylvania Constitutional Convention. As president of the convention, he helped draft a new state constitution that embodied the principles of democracy and individual rights. The Pennsylvania Constitution of 1776 was one of the most progressive documents of its time. It included provisions for a unicameral legislature*, annual elections, and broader suffrage rights than those found in many other states. Benjamin's vision for the constitution emphasized the importance of a government that was accountable to its citizens and protected their fundamental liberties. His efforts ensured that Pennsylvania's new government reflected Enlightenment ideals and set a precedent for other states to follow.

Simultaneously, Benjamin was appointed to a committee of five tasked with drafting the Declaration of Independence. Working alongside Thomas Jefferson, John Adams, Roger Sherman, and Robert R. Livingston, Benjamin contributed to what would become one of the most significant documents in American history. The Declaration of Independence articulated the colonies' grievances against the British Crown and asserted their right to self-governance. Benjamin's diplomatic prowess and persuasive arguments were instrumental in securing consensus among the delegates, ensuring that the declaration presented a united front to the world. His experience and wisdom helped refine Jefferson's draft, adding gravitas and clarity to the final document.

Benjamin's contributions did not stop at the drafting of foundational

---

\* A unicameral legislature, also known as unicameralism, is a type of legislature consisting of a single house or assembly that legislates and votes as one body.

documents. Later that year, he was appointed as one of the Commissioners of Congress to the French Court, a mission critical to the American struggle for independence. Arriving in Paris on December 21, 1776, Benjamin's primary objective was to secure French support for the American cause. This support was essential, as the fledgling United States needed military aid, financial assistance, and international recognition to sustain its fight against Britain.

Benjamin's charm, wit, and intellect quickly endeared him to the French aristocracy and intellectuals. His reputation as a scientist and philosopher, combined with his approachable demeanor, made him a highly effective diplomat. He cultivated relationships with key figures such as the Comte de Vergennes, the French Foreign Minister, and King Louis XVI. Benjamin's ability to navigate the complex social and political landscape of the French court was remarkable. He attended salons, engaged in intellectual discussions, and used his scientific achievements to build rapport with influential individuals.

One of Benjamin's most important allies was Jacques-Donatien Le Ray de Chaumont, a wealthy French merchant and supporter of the American cause. Le Ray provided Benjamin with financial support and logistical assistance, facilitating the shipment of arms and supplies to the American forces. Benjamin's relationship with Le Ray exemplified his ability to forge strategic partnerships that advanced the interests of the United States.

Benjamin's diplomatic efforts culminated in the signing of the Treaty of Alliance with France in 1778. This treaty formalized French military and financial support for the American Revolution, marking a turning point in the conflict. The alliance with France provided the Continental Army with much-needed resources and reinforcements, significantly bolstering their chances of success against the British. Benjamin's role in securing this alliance cannot be overstated; his skillful diplomacy and ability to win the trust and admiration of the French were crucial to the treaty's success.

Throughout his time in France, Benjamin also maintained extensive correspondence with key American leaders, keeping them informed of developments and offering strategic advice. His letters to Congress and other figures were filled with insights and recommendations based on his experiences and observations in Europe. Benjamin's ability to balance his diplomatic duties with his role as a communicator and strategist demonstrated his exceptional dedication to the American cause.

In addition to his formal diplomatic duties, Benjamin's presence in France had a profound impact on public opinion. He became a symbol of the American struggle for liberty, embodying the Enlightenment values of reason, science, and democratic governance. His iconic fur hat and plain dress stood in stark contrast to the opulence of the French court, reinforcing the image of America as a land of simplicity and virtue. This carefully crafted persona helped garner widespread sympathy and support for the American Revolution among the French populace.

He faced long periods of separation from his family, health issues, and the constant pressure of navigating complex political dynamics.

The relationship with his son William also began to become increasingly strained. In 1763, William was appointed as the Royal Governor of New Jersey, a prestigious position that solidified his loyalty to the British Crown. However, as tensions between the American colonies and Britain escalated, William's steadfast support for British authority placed him in direct conflict with his father's growing revolutionary fervor. Despite Benjamin Franklin's pivotal role in the American Revolution, William remained a staunch Loyalist, believing in the necessity of maintaining colonial ties to Britain for stability and prosperity. This divergence in political allegiance strained their relationship, culminating in William's arrest by American forces in 1776 and subsequent imprisonment. After the war, William moved to England, where he continued to advocate for Loyalist causes, ultimately spending the rest of his life in exile. William's shifting loyalties resulted in estrangement with Benjamin that deepened during this time.

The stress of estrangement from his son and the distance from his other loved ones took a significant toll on Benjamin's well-being, exacerbating his health challenges during this particularly hard period. He suffered from gout, a painful form of arthritis caused by the accumulation of uric acid crystals in the joints, which frequently incapacitated him. The condition often left him bedridden for days or even weeks at a time, significantly impacting his ability to travel and attend meetings. Additionally, Benjamin experienced recurrent episodes of kidney stones, which caused excruciating pain and required careful management. Despite these harsh ailments, Benjamin's resilience and determination allowed him to continue his vital work, balancing his diplomatic duties with the need to manage his health.

These physical ailments were compounded by the emotional strain of being away from his family. Benjamin missed significant events in the lives of his children and grandchildren, and he deeply felt the absence of his daughter, Sally, and her family. The letters he exchanged with them reveal a man who, despite his immense responsibilities and public persona, remained profoundly connected to his loved ones and yearned for their companionship.

Benjamin's health issues did not diminish his effectiveness as a diplomat, but they did add a layer of complexity to his already challenging role. Navigating the intricacies of French court politics and securing support for the American cause required constant engagement and sharp intellect, both of which were made more difficult by his physical suffering. Nonetheless, Benjamin's ability to persevere through these hardships and maintain his focus on the larger goal of American independence is a testament to his extraordinary character and dedication.

In 1777, during his time in France, Benjamin Franklin, who was seventy-one years old, met Madame Anne-Louise Brillon de Jouy, who was thirty-three years old. They developed a close and affectionate relationship, bonded by their shared intellectual pursuits and mutual respect. Madame Brillon was known for her musical talents, intellectual prowess, and vibrant salon, which attracted some of the most influential thinkers and artists of the time. Their correspondence and interactions provided Benjamin with a much-needed personal respite from his demanding diplomatic duties. Madame Brillon's companionship and their intellectual exchanges enriched Benjamin's time in France, offering him a sense of connection and comfort amidst the pressures of his diplomatic mission.

Benjamin's relationship with Madame Brillon went beyond mere friendship; it was a meeting of minds that stimulated both intellectually and emotionally. They exchanged letters frequently, discussing a wide range of topics from philosophy and science to politics and personal reflections. These letters reveal a deep mutual respect and affection, as well as a shared love of music and culture. Madame Brillon's home became a sanctuary for Benjamin, where he could relax and enjoy stimulating conversations, music, and a warm, supportive atmosphere.

In 1778, Benjamin's tireless diplomatic efforts bore fruit when he signed the Treaty of Alliance with France. This pivotal agreement formalized French military and financial support for the American Revolution, dramatically altering the balance of power and providing the colonies with the resources necessary to continue their fight against Britain. The treaty was a monumental achievement, as it marked the first formal recognition of the United States as an independent nation by a major European power. The French alliance was a turning point in the war, demonstrating Benjamin's unparalleled diplomatic skills and his ability to secure crucial international support.

The alliance with France brought significant benefits to the American cause. French financial aid helped sustain the Continental Army, while French troops and naval forces provided critical military support. The presence of the French fleet in American waters challenged British naval supremacy and played a decisive role in key battles, such as the Battle of Yorktown in 1781. Benjamin's success in securing this alliance underscored his importance as a diplomat and his ability to navigate complex international relationships.

Between 1779 and 1781, Benjamin was appointed to negotiate a peace treaty with England. His deep understanding of both

American and British perspectives, coupled with his diplomatic acumen, made him an indispensable figure in the peace negotiations. Benjamin's contributions to the drafting and signing of the Treaty of Paris in 1783 ultimately brought an end to the Revolutionary War and secured American independence. His role in these negotiations underscored his importance as a statesman and his commitment to the principles of liberty and justice.

Benjamin's role in the peace negotiations was characterized by his strategic insight and ability to build consensus among diverse parties. The negotiations involved representatives from the United States, Great Britain, France, and Spain, each with their own interests and objectives. Benjamin's ability to navigate these complexities and find common ground was crucial in achieving a successful outcome. His diplomatic skills were instrumental in securing favorable terms for the United States, including recognition of American independence, the establishment of borders, and the resolution of debts and property claims.

Benjamin's contributions to the Treaty of Paris were a culmination of his lifelong dedication to the cause of American independence. His tireless efforts, both in securing international support and in negotiating the terms of peace, were critical in achieving the ultimate goal of liberty and self-governance for the American people. The successful conclusion of the Revolutionary War and the establishment of the United States as an independent nation were testaments to Benjamin's vision, perseverance, and extraordinary diplomatic talent.

Throughout his time in France, Benjamin's health continued to be a challenge, but his resilience and determination never wavered. He remained committed to his diplomatic duties, despite the personal sacrifices and physical ailments he endured. His ability to balance these demands while maintaining his intellectual and social engagements, such as his relationship with Madame Brillon, highlights the depth of his character and his unwavering dedication to his country.

Benjamin's later years in France were also marked by his continued engagement in scientific and intellectual pursuits. He remained a

 prominent figure in the French Enlightenment community, corresponding with leading philosophers and scientists. Benjamin's time in France solidified his legacy as a transatlantic figure who bridged the worlds of politics, science, and philosophy.

Reflecting on his long and varied career, Benjamin began to see the fruition of his lifelong dedication to public service, scientific inquiry, and the pursuit of knowledge. His autobiography, which he continued to write in intervals, encapsulated the wisdom and experiences he had gathered over the decades. Benjamin's autobiography is a candid reflection of his life's journey, providing valuable insights into his thoughts, philosophies, and personal growth. In the book, he chronicled his humble beginnings in Boston, detailing his early life, family background, and the formative years that shaped his character. He recounted his apprenticeship with his brother James, his eventual escape to Philadelphia, and his rise to prominence as a printer, scientist, and statesman.

Benjamin's autobiography not only recounted the events of his life; he also presented his guide to personal development and ethical living. He shared the various challenges and triumphs he encountered, offering lessons drawn from his own experiences. One of the most notable aspects of the autobiography is his inclusion of the thirteen virtues, a set of principles he devised to cultivate moral character and personal discipline. These virtues are:

1. **Temperance**: Eat not to dullness; drink not to elevation.
2. **Silence**: Speak not but what may benefit others or yourself; avoid trifling conversation.
3. **Order**: Let all your things have their places; let each part of your business have its time.
4. **Resolution**: Resolve to perform what you ought; perform without fail what you resolve.
5. **Frugality**: Make no expense but to do good to others or yourself; waste nothing.

6. **Industry**: Lose no time; be always employed in something useful; cut off all unnecessary actions.
7. **Sincerity**: Use no hurtful deceit; think innocently and justly, and, if you speak, speak accordingly.
8. **Justice**: Wrong none by doing injuries, or omitting the benefits that are your duty.
9. **Moderation**: Avoid extremes; forbear resenting injuries so much as you think they deserve.
10. **Cleanliness**: Tolerate no uncleanliness in body, clothes, or habitation.
11. **Tranquility**: Be not disturbed at trifles, or at accidents common or unavoidable.
12. **Chastity**: Rarely use venery but for health or offspring, never to dullness, weakness, or the injury of your own or another's peace or reputation.
13. **Humility**: Imitate Jesus and Socrates.

Benjamin's dedication to these virtues was a testament to his commitment to self-improvement and ethical living. He devised a method to track his adherence to these principles, creating a chart where he marked his progress, aiming to perfect each virtue one at a time. This disciplined approach to personal growth is one of the key themes in his autobiography, highlighting his belief in the importance of moral integrity and continuous self-betterment.

As Benjamin approached the final chapters of his life, his contributions to the American Revolution and his enduring influence on both sides of the Atlantic became increasingly evident. His legacy was not just that of a Founding Father of the United States, but also of a pioneering scientist, a gifted diplomat, and a philosopher who embodied the Enlightenment ideals of reason and progress. Benjamin's journey from a young printer in Philadelphia to a revered statesman and intellectual giant was a testament to his extraordinary talents and unwavering dedication to the betterment of society.

## 6. Architect of Independence

In the latter part of his life, despite personal disappointments and health challenges, Benjamin continued to make significant contributions that would leave a lasting impact on the emerging United States and the world.

As the American Revolution drew to a close, Benjamin Franklin remained in France, playing a critical role in the negotiations that would bring about the end of the war. His diplomatic skills, honed over decades of public service, were pivotal in securing a favorable peace for the fledgling United States. The culmination of these efforts was the Treaty of Paris, signed on September 3, 1783, by Benjamin, John Adams, and John Jay on behalf of the United States, and by David Hartley for Great Britain.

The path to the Treaty of Paris was complex and fraught with challenges. The American commissioners faced not only the British but also the interests of their French and Spanish allies, who had their own objectives in the post-war settlement. Benjamin's primary task was to balance these competing interests while securing the most advantageous terms for the United States.

Negotiations began in earnest in 1782, after the British defeat at Yorktown in 1781 had made it clear that they could not win the war. The American commissioners, led by Benjamin, had to navigate a series of diplomatic hurdles. The French, under Foreign Minister Comte de Vergennes, sought to limit American expansion westward, preferring a weaker United States that would be more dependent on French support. Meanwhile, the Spanish were concerned about their own territorial claims in North America.

Benjamin's experience, charm, and strategic acumen were critical in these negotiations. He leveraged his long-standing relationships with key French officials and used his deep understanding of European politics to counterbalance French and Spanish interests. At the same time, he worked closely with Adams and Jay to ensure a unified American negotiating stance.

One of the major issues was the recognition of American independence. While the British were willing to admit this point, the terms of peace would determine the future strength and territorial reach of the new nation. Benjamin and his colleagues insisted on boundaries that would allow for American expansion and economic growth. They aimed to secure not only independence but also the resources necessary for the United States to thrive.

The final terms of the Treaty of Paris were highly favorable to the United States. Britain recognized the independence of the United States and agreed to boundaries that extended from the Atlantic Ocean to the Mississippi River, and from Canada in the north to Spanish Florida in the south. This vast territory provided the new nation with ample land for expansion, resources for economic development, and strategic depth.

Additionally, the treaty addressed several other critical issues. It granted Americans fishing rights off the coast of Newfoundland and in the Gulf of Saint Lawrence, which were vital to the New England economy. It also stipulated the withdrawal of British troops from American territory, although this process would prove to be slower and more complicated than anticipated. The treaty further provided for the fair treatment of American loyalists, though this provision would lead to considerable tension and disputes in the post-war period.

Benjamin's role in these negotiations cannot be overstated. His diplomatic finesse and ability to build consensus were crucial in achieving a treaty that not only ended the war but also laid a strong foundation for the future growth and stability of the United States. His contributions to the Treaty of Paris underscored his importance as a statesman and his commitment to the principles of liberty and justice.

The successful negotiation of the Treaty of Paris was a monumental achievement that highlighted Benjamin's unique blend of pragmatism and idealism. It demonstrated his skill in navigating complex international relations and his unwavering dedication to securing the best possible outcome for his country. Benjamin's work in France during this period was the capstone of his diplomatic career and a testament to his enduring impact on the founding of the United States.

As Benjamin prepared to return to America, the significance of the Treaty of Paris was clear. It marked the end of a long and tiring struggle for independence and the beginning of a new chapter in American history. The favorable terms of the treaty provided the United States with the territorial, economic, and political resources needed to build a strong and prosperous nation. Benjamin's role in securing these terms ensured that his legacy would be remembered not only as a Founding Father but also as a master diplomat who played a pivotal role in shaping the destiny of the United States.

Benjamin's return to America was met with widespread acclaim and gratitude. He was celebrated as a hero who had helped to secure the nation's future through his tireless efforts in France. The Treaty of Paris was a crowning achievement in a life marked by remarkable accomplishments, and it solidified Benjamin's place as one of the most important figures in American history.

While Benjamin's public successes were evident, his personal life experienced moments of deep longing and disappointment. During his time in France, Benjamin developed a close relationship with

Madame Anne-Catherine de Lignville Helvétius, a charming and intelligent widow known for her vibrant salon that attracted some of the greatest minds of the time. Benjamin, captivated by her wit and intellect, proposed marriage to Madame Helvétius. However, she  graciously rejected his offer, preferring to remain independent and maintain the life she had built. Despite this rejection, Benjamin cherished their friendship and continued to enjoy her company, finding solace and companionship in their intellectual exchanges.

In the years following the signing of the Treaty of Paris in 1783, Benjamin Franklin returned to America in 1785, at the age of seventy-nine. He brought with him not only the experience and accolades of his diplomatic triumphs but also an undiminished passion for scientific inquiry and innovation. Resuming his scientific and political endeavors with characteristic vigor, Benjamin continued to explore ways to solve everyday problems through practical inventions.

One of his most notable contributions during this period was the invention of bifocals in 1784. As Benjamin aged, he, like many others, experienced presbyopia, a common condition where the eyes gradually lose the ability to focus on close objects. This condition required him to constantly switch between different pairs of glasses for reading and for seeing at a distance, which he found inconvenient.

Driven by his desire for a practical solution, Benjamin devised bifocals, a revolutionary innovation that combined two different optical lenses into a single frame. The upper part of the lens corrected for distance vision, while the lower part corrected for near vision. This design allowed the wearer to see clearly at multiple distances without the need to change glasses. By simply tilting their head, users could switch from reading a book to looking across the room, significantly enhancing their daily lives.

Benjamin's return to America also marked his re-engagement with political life. In 1785, he was elected President of the Pennsylvania Executive Council, a role equivalent to that of a modern-day governor. Benjamin's leadership in this position was marked by his efforts to promote economic development, education, and civic improvements. He used his influence to advocate for the construction of new roads, the improvement of public schools, and the establishment of better systems for public health and safety.

During this period, Benjamin continued to innovate. In 1786, he invented the "long arm," a simple but effective instrument for retrieving books from high shelves. This device consisted of a wooden pole with a grasping mechanism at one end, allowing users to reach and securely grab books that were otherwise out of reach. The invention of the long arm reflected Benjamin's lifelong commitment to making knowledge more accessible and his knack for creating practical solutions to everyday challenges.

Benjamin's political and scientific achievements were paralleled by his involvement in shaping the foundational structures of the United States. In 1787, he played a pivotal role in the Constitutional Convention, where he was one of the signatories of the United States Constitution. His wisdom, experience, and ability to mediate between conflicting viewpoints were invaluable during the drafting process. Benjamin's signature on the Constitution represented not only his endorsement of the new framework of government but also his belief in the principles of democracy, federalism, and the protection of individual rights.

Despite his advancing age and declining health, Benjamin Franklin remained an active and vocal advocate for social justice. At the age of eighty-three, in 1789, he penned a significant anti-slavery treatise, passionately arguing for the abolition of slavery and the recognition of the inherent rights of all individuals. This powerful document was a reflection of Benjamin's evolving views on slavery, illustrating a profound transformation in his perspective and his unwavering commitment to the principles of liberty and human dignity.

Benjamin's early life and career were marked by the norms of his time, including the acceptance and practice of slavery. Like many of his contemporaries, he owned slaves and benefited from their labor. However, over the years, Benjamin's views began to change, influenced by his exposure to Enlightenment ideals and his growing recognition of the inherent contradictions between the principles of freedom and the practice of slavery.

Throughout the latter part of his life, Benjamin became increasingly associated with abolitionist thinkers and organizations. His involvement with the Pennsylvania Society for Promoting the Abolition of Slavery, one of the first abolitionist groups in America, was particularly significant. Founded in 1775, the society aimed to end slavery and promote the rights and welfare of freed African Americans. Benjamin became an active member and, in 1787, was elected its president.

Benjamin's anti-slavery treatise of 1789, titled *An Address to the Public*, was a culmination of his commitment to the abolitionist cause. In this document, he laid out a compelling moral and ethical argument against slavery, emphasizing the fundamental rights of all human beings to liberty and justice. Benjamin drew upon his extensive knowledge of history, philosophy, and religion to condemn the institution of slavery as inherently unjust and inhumane.

The treatise began by acknowledging the historical prevalence of slavery but argued that its existence did not justify its continuation. Benjamin highlighted the brutal realities of slavery, including the physical and psychological suffering endured by enslaved individuals. He condemned the hypocrisy of a nation founded on the ideals of liberty and equality while simultaneously denying these rights to a significant portion of its population.

Benjamin's argument extended beyond the immediate moral issues, addressing the long-term societal and economic implications of slavery. He contended that a society built on the principles of justice and equality would be stronger, more prosperous, and more harmonious. By abolishing slavery, America could align its practices with its founding ideals and set a powerful example for the rest of the world.

Benjamin's treatise also included practical recommendations for the abolition of slavery. He advocated for gradual emancipation, a strategy designed to address the complexities and resistance associated with immediate abolition. This approach aimed to prepare society for the transition and provide opportunities for the integration of freed individuals into the economic and social fabric of the nation.

In addition to his writings, Benjamin's leadership within the Pennsylvania Society for Promoting the Abolition of Slavery was instrumental in advancing the cause. Under his guidance, the society engaged in various activities, including public advocacy, education, and legal assistance for freed African Americans. The society worked to challenge the legal and social structures that supported slavery, promoting legislation that would pave the way for its eventual abolition.

Benjamin's anti-slavery efforts were part of a broader movement that included other prominent figures of the time, such as Thomas Paine, John Jay, and Alexander Hamilton. These individuals, inspired by the same Enlightenment ideals that had influenced Benjamin, sought to create a society where the rights of all individuals were respected and protected. Benjamin's contributions added significant weight to the movement, given his stature and influence as a Founding Father and respected statesman.

Benjamin's commitment to the abolitionist cause extended beyond his writings. Under Benjamin's leadership, the society worked to raise public awareness about the injustices of slavery and to lobby for legislative changes that would lead to its eventual eradication.

Throughout these years, Benjamin's health was a constant concern. He suffered from severe gout and other ailments, which often left him bedridden and in great pain. Despite these physical challenges, his mental faculties remained sharp, and he continued to correspond with friends, fellow scientists, and political leaders. His letters from this period reflect a man deeply engaged with the issues of his time, offering insights and advice on a wide range of topics.

Benjamin's final years were marked by a blend of public service, scientific inquiry, and personal reflection. He continued to write, invent, and advocate for causes he believed in, leaving behind a legacy that would influence generations to come. His contributions to the fields of science, politics, and social justice were vast and varied, underscoring his role as one of the most remarkable figures in American history.

In April 1790, Benjamin Franklin passed away at the age of eighty-four, marking the end of a life filled with remarkable achievements and contributions to society. His death was not only a significant loss for America but was also mourned in France and other parts of the world where his influence had been profoundly felt. The international grief underscored the global reach of Benjamin's legacy as a statesman, scientist, and philosopher.

Benjamin's health had been declining for several years before his death. He suffered from a range of ailments, including gout and kidney stones, which caused him considerable pain and discomfort. In his final months, Benjamin was bedridden and struggled with severe complications from pleurisy, an inflammation of the tissues surrounding the lungs. On April 17, 1790, Benjamin Franklin succumbed to his illnesses and died peacefully at his home in Philadelphia.

In Philadelphia, the city that had been the epicenter of many of Benjamin's endeavors, thousands of people gathered to pay their respects. His funeral procession was a grand event, reflecting the high esteem in which he was held by his contemporaries. Citizens from all walks of life, including prominent figures in politics, science, and business, joined the throng of mourners. The streets were lined with people, and the outpouring of grief and respect demonstrated the deep affection and admiration that the public had for Benjamin.

The ceremony itself was marked by numerous tributes to Benjamin's life and work. Eulogies highlighted his numerous contributions to the American Revolution, his pivotal role in drafting the Declaration of Independence, and his diplomatic efforts that helped secure crucial alliances during the Revolutionary War. Speakers also celebrated his scientific innovations, such as the lightning rod, bifocals, and the Benjamin stove, which had significantly improved everyday life for many.

Benjamin's passing marked a solemn moment in history, as it was the loss of one of the last remaining Founding Fathers of the United States. His death prompted reflections on his extraordinary life — a life that exemplified the Enlightenment ideals of reason, inquiry, and progress. Benjamin's intellectual curiosity had driven him to explore and understand the natural world, leading to significant advancements in science and technology.

Moreover, Benjamin's practical innovations were a testament to his belief in applying knowledge for the betterment of society. His invention of the lightning rod had saved countless buildings from destruction, while his development of bifocals improved the quality of life for many individuals with vision problems. Benjamin's dedication to public service was also evident in his establishment of institutions such as the first public library in America and the University of Pennsylvania.

Benjamin's unwavering commitment to the principles of liberty and justice was a cornerstone of his legacy. Throughout his life, he had advocated for the rights and freedoms of individuals, speaking out against tyranny and oppression. His later years were marked by a strong stance against slavery, culminating in his presidency of the Society for Promoting the Abolition of Slavery and his powerful anti-slavery writings. This shift in his views demonstrated his ability to grow and adapt his beliefs in light of new understandings and moral considerations.

Internationally, Benjamin's death was noted by many leaders and intellectuals who recognized his contributions to the global Enlightenment movement. In France, where he had spent significant time securing support for the American Revolution, his passing was particularly felt. French intellectuals and political leaders, who had been inspired by Benjamin's ideas and diplomatic efforts, mourned the loss of a kindred spirit and a key figure in the transatlantic exchange of ideas. His contributions to fostering the Franco-American alliance had left an indelible mark on the history of both nations.

## 7. The Enduring Legacy

Benjamin Franklin's legacy is rich and filled with contributions to science, politics, and society. His story woven with the threads of his enduring influence and thoughtful bequests*. As one of the most prominent Founding Fathers of the United States, Benjamin's impact extends far beyond his own time, with his likeness, ideas, and innovations continuing to shape the world today.

In the final years of his life, Benjamin made provisions to ensure that his influence would benefit future generations. One of his most notable bequests was to the cities of Boston and Philadelphia. Inspired by a parody written by the French mathematician Charles-Joseph Mathon de la Cour, Benjamin decided to leave £1,000

---

\* A bequest is a gift of personal property, money, or assets that is left to someone in a will. It typically refers to items or funds that are designated to be given to beneficiaries after the person who made the will (the testator) has passed away. Bequests can include cash, securities, jewelry, real estate, and other valuables, and they are a common way for individuals to distribute their estate according to their wishes.

(approximately $4,400 at the time, or about $125,000 in today's dollars) to each city, with instructions for the money to gather interest over 200 years. This idea stemmed from the parody's character who left a small amount of money to collect interest over several centuries, resulting in vast sums for utopian projects.

Benjamin's bequests, initiated in 1785, were a visionary act of philanthropy that illustrated his profound foresight and commitment to the future welfare of society. By the time the trust matured in 1990, the Philadelphia fund had accumulated more than $2,000,000. This remarkable growth was due to Benjamin's ingenious use of compound interest, which he understood would significantly increase the funds over two centuries. From 1940 to 1990, the trust was primarily utilized for mortgage loans, providing local residents with financial assistance to purchase homes and contribute to the stability and growth of the community.

When the trust finally matured, Philadelphia made a pivotal decision to allocate the accumulated funds toward scholarships for local high school students. This initiative not only honored Benjamin's legacy of education and public service but also provided countless young individuals with the opportunity to pursue higher education, thereby fostering a new generation of informed and engaged citizens. By investing in education, Philadelphia ensured that Benjamin's vision for community development and empowerment continued to thrive.

In Boston, the trust fund experienced similar growth, reaching nearly $5,000,000 by 1990. Initially, a portion of these funds were used to establish a trade school, which was a direct reflection of Benjamin's practical approach to education and his belief in equipping individuals with skills that would be valuable in the workforce. This trade school eventually evolved into the Franklin Institute of Boston, an institution dedicated to advancing education in the fields of science, engineering, and technology. Over time, the entire trust fund was dedicated to supporting this institute, ensuring that Benjamin's legacy of promoting practical education and scientific inquiry lived on.

In 1787, Benjamin's legacy was further cemented when a group of prominent ministers in Lancaster, Pennsylvania, proposed the foundation of a new college named in his honor. Benjamin contributed £200 toward the development of Franklin College, a substantial amount equivalent to approximately $28,000 in today's money. This significant donation and his ongoing support for the college underscored his dedication to higher education and the cultivation of knowledge.

Franklin College eventually merged with Marshall College to become Franklin & Marshall College, an institution that continues to thrive and honor Benjamin's commitment to learning. By supporting the establishment of this college, Benjamin demonstrated his belief in the transformative power of education and his desire to ensure that future generations would have access to quality learning opportunities. His donation not only helped lay the financial foundation for the college but also served as a testament to his enduring legacy in the field of education.

Benjamin's likeness and image have become ever present symbols of American heritage and creativity. As the only person to have signed the Declaration of Independence in 1776, the Treaty of Alliance with France in 1778, the Treaty of Paris in 1783, and the US Constitution in 1787, Benjamin is often considered one of the foremost Founding Fathers. This unique distinction has led to his being jocularly referred to as "the only president of the United States who was never president of the United States."

Since 1914, Benjamin's portrait has adorned the $100 bill, a testament to his lasting impact on American culture and finance. From 1948 to 1963, his likeness also appeared on the half-dollar coin. Additionally, he has been featured on a $50 bill and several versions of the $100 bill from 1914 and 1918, as well as the $1,000 Series EE savings bond. Benjamin's image on currency serves as a constant reminder of his contributions to the nation's founding and his enduring legacy in American history.

Benjamin has also been honored with numerous memorials and statues. On April 12, 1976, as part of the bicentennial* celebration, Congress dedicated a twenty-foot-tall marble statue at Philadelphia's Franklin Institute, known as the Benjamin Franklin National Memorial. This statue, presided over by Vice President Nelson Rockefeller at the dedication ceremony, stands as a tribute to Benjamin's lasting influence. The Franklin Institute also houses many of Benjamin's personal possessions, providing visitors with a glimpse into his life and achievements.

In London, Benjamin's house at 36 Craven Street, the only surviving former residence of Benjamin, has been preserved and opened to the public as the Benjamin Franklin House. Marked initially with a blue plaque, the house now serves as a museum dedicated to Benjamin's life and work. In 1998, during restoration work, the remains of six children and four adults were discovered buried under the house. These remains were likely placed there by William Hewson, a friend of Benjamin who had built an anatomy school at the back of the house. While Benjamin likely knew of Hewson's activities, there is no evidence to suggest he participated in the dissections, as his interests were more aligned with physics and other sciences.

Benjamin has also been commemorated on US postage stamps more frequently than any other American figure except George Washington. His image first appeared on a US postage stamp in 1847, and from 1908 through 1923, the US Post Office issued a series of stamps commonly referred to as the Washington–Franklin Issues, featuring both Washington and Benjamin in various denominations. These stamps, which ran for fourteen years, represent the longest series in US postal history, underscoring Benjamin's significant role in American history. Despite this

---

* The term "bicentennial" refers to the 200th anniversary of a significant event. It is derived from the Latin words "bi-" meaning two and "centennial" meaning a period of 100 years. Bicentennial celebrations often involve commemorations, events, and activities that reflect on the historical importance of the event being remembered and celebrate its legacy over the past two centuries. For example, the United States celebrated its bicentennial in 1976, marking 200 years since the signing of the Declaration of Independence in 1776.

extensive representation, Benjamin only appears on a few commemorative stamps, but the engravings on these stamps are considered some of the finest portrayals of him on record.

Benjamin's contributions to society, science, and politics have been celebrated and remembered in countless ways. His inventions, such as bifocals and the lightning rod, have had lasting impacts on everyday life. In 1784, Benjamin invented bifocals to address the common problem of presbyopia, or age-related difficulty in focusing on close objects. The invention of bifocals exemplifies Benjamin's ability to apply scientific principles to practical problems, improving the daily lives of countless individuals.

In 1789, he wrote an anti-slavery treatise, passionately arguing for the abolition of slavery and the recognition of the inherent rights of all individuals. This treatise was a reflection of Benjamin's evolving views on slavery; although he had once owned slaves, he had become a staunch abolitionist in his later years, recognizing the profound moral and ethical issues posed by the institution of slavery. His anti-slavery efforts culminated in his presidency of the Society for Promoting the Abolition of Slavery, where he worked tirelessly to raise public awareness and promote legislative changes aimed at ending slavery.

Benjamin's legacy is also preserved through the numerous statues and memorials erected in his honor. A life-size bronze statue of Benjamin seated with a cane can be found in the National Constitution Center in Philadelphia. This statue, along with others, serves as a reminder of Benjamin's enduring contributions to the founding and shaping of the United States.

In popular media, Benjamin Franklin's life and achievements have been portrayed in various films, television series, and books, each capturing different facets of his multifaceted character. He is often depicted as a wise and witty statesman, a brilliant inventor, and a shrewd diplomat. These portrayals highlight his significant impact on American history and culture, bringing his remarkable contributions to a broader audience.

One notable example is the 2008 miniseries *John Adams*, produced by HBO, where Benjamin is portrayed by Tom Wilkinson. The series, based on David McCullough's biography of John Adams, vividly depicts Benjamin's diplomatic efforts in France during the American Revolution, showcasing his wit, charm, and strategic acumen. Wilkinson's portrayal captures Benjamin's complex personality and his crucial role in securing French support for the American cause.

In the 1974 television special *Ben and Me*, an animated short film by Disney, Benjamin's life is humorously narrated through the perspective of a mouse named Amos. While the story is fictional, it creatively introduces younger audiences to Benjamin's inventions and his contributions to American independence, highlighting his innovative spirit and the whimsical aspects of his character.

The 2002 film *Liberty's Kids*, an animated historical fiction television series, also features Benjamin Franklin as a central character, voiced by actor Walter Cronkite. The series is aimed at educating children about the American Revolution through the eyes of young journalists who interact with historical figures. Benjamin's character serves as a mentor and provides wisdom and guidance, emphasizing his role as a Founding Father and his commitment to education and enlightenment values.

Literature has also provided rich portrayals of Benjamin. In historical novels like *The First American: The Life and Times of Benjamin Franklin* by H.W. Brands, readers gain a comprehensive view of Benjamin's life, exploring his journey from a young apprentice to a revered statesman. The book delves into his scientific achievements, political endeavors, and personal philosophies, offering an in-depth understanding of his contributions to the formation of the United States.

In the realm of nonfiction, *Benjamin Franklin: An American Life* by Walter Isaacson provides a detailed biography that examines Benjamin's diverse talents and his profound influence on American society. Isaacson's work highlights Benjamin's role in drafting the

Declaration of Independence, negotiating the Treaty of Paris, and shaping the US Constitution, painting a vivid picture of his diplomatic and intellectual prowess.

Moreover, Benjamin's essays and writings, such as his autobiography and *Poor Richard's Almanack*, continue to be celebrated for their insight and humor. These works reveal his practical wisdom and his belief in self-improvement, thrift, and hard work, values that have resonated with generations of readers.

Benjamin's legacy has even extended to the digital age. In video games like *Assassin's Creed III*, set during the American Revolution, Benjamin appears as a character, introducing players to his inventions and political ideas within the game's historical narrative. This modern portrayal helps to engage younger audiences and spark interest in Benjamin's life and the era he helped shape.

These various portrayals across media underscore Benjamin Franklin's enduring influence and the fascination with his life and achievements. Whether depicted in films, television series, books, or video games, Benjamin's legacy as a wise statesman, inventive genius, and diplomatic leader continues to captivate and educate audiences around the world.

Benjamin's influence extends beyond his lifetime, as his ideas and innovations continue to inspire and shape modern society. His emphasis on education, civic engagement, and scientific inquiry remains relevant today, and his legacy as a Founding Father and pioneer of enlightenment values endures.

# Conclusion

Benjamin Franklin's life story is a testament to the power of curiosity, perseverance, and civic duty. As one of the most influential figures in American history, Benjamin's contributions span across various domains, including science, politics, literature, and social reform. His innovative spirit and relentless pursuit of knowledge not only shaped the emerging United States but also left a lasting impact on the world.

From his humble beginnings as a printer's apprentice to his pivotal role in the founding of a new nation, Benjamin's journey is marked by a series of remarkable achievements. His inventions, such as the lightning rod and bifocals, revolutionized daily life and demonstrated his ability to apply scientific principles to practical problems. As a diplomat, Benjamin's efforts in securing French support during the American Revolution and negotiating the Treaty of Paris were crucial in achieving American independence. His wisdom and leadership in the drafting of the Declaration of Independence and the US Constitution helped lay the foundation for the democratic principles that continue to guide the nation.

Benjamin's legacy is also reflected in his lifelong commitment to education and social justice. His founding of institutions like the Library Company of Philadelphia and the University of

Pennsylvania underscored his belief in the transformative power of knowledge. His evolving views on slavery, culminating in his passionate advocacy for abolition, highlight his dedication to the principles of liberty and equality.

Throughout his life, Benjamin remained a figure of enduring curiosity and intellect. His autobiography, filled with reflections and advice, offers invaluable insights into the mindset of one of America's Founding Fathers. Benjamin's ability to balance his numerous roles – scientist, inventor, statesman, writer, and philosopher – demonstrates the breadth of his talents and his unwavering commitment to the betterment of society.

As we reflect on Benjamin's legacy, it is clear that his contributions continue to resonate today. His emphasis on education, civic engagement, and scientific inquiry remains relevant, inspiring future generations to pursue knowledge and innovation. Benjamin's life serves as a reminder of the profound impact that one individual can have on the course of history through dedication, ingenuity, and a relentless pursuit of progress.

In the end, Benjamin Franklin's story is not just about the accomplishments of one man, but about the enduring spirit of curiosity and the quest for a better world. His life and legacy remind us that through hard work, determination, and a commitment to the common good, we can leave an indelible mark on the world, much like Benjamin did. As we look to the future, let us draw inspiration from his example and strive to embody the principles that guided him throughout his remarkable journey.

# Appendices

### A. Chronological Timeline of Benjamin Franklin's Life

**1706**

- January 17: Born in Boston, the youngest son of Josiah and Abiah (Folger) Franklin.

**1715**

- Completes his final formal year of schooling.

**1717**

- Begins reading Plutarch, Defoe, and Cotton Mather.
- Briefly indentured as a cutler.

**1718**

- Apprenticed to his brother James, a printer.
- Writes a ballad to mark the capture of Blackbeard the Pirate.

**1720**

- Moves away from home into a boarding house.
- Stops attending church to use Sundays for study.

## 1721

- Brother James Franklin starts publishing *The New England Courant*.
- Boston faces a smallpox epidemic and vaccination controversy.

## 1722

- Becomes a vegetarian to save money for books and due to a distaste for flesh.

## 1723

- Takes over publishing *The Courant* after brother James is jailed.
- Runs away from his apprenticeship and travels to New York, then to Philadelphia, where he gains employment as a printer.
- Takes lodging with John Read, whose daughter Deborah will become his wife in 1730.

## 1724

- Courts Deborah Read and, under encouragement from Philadelphia Governor William Keith, travels to London to buy printing equipment. Keith's letters of credit never materialize, and Benjamin is stranded in London, working for Samuel Palmer as a printer.

## 1725

- Publishes his first pamphlet: *A Dissertation upon Liberty and Necessity, Pleasure and Pain*.
- Leaves Palmer's shop for a larger one run by John Watts.
- Attends theater, reads voraciously, and frequents coffee houses.
- Deborah Read marries John Rogers in August.

**1726**

- Returns to Philadelphia in July and works for Thomas Denham, a merchant, as a bookkeeper and shopkeeper in a store selling imported clothes and hardware.

**1727**

- Suffers his first pleurisy attack.
- Leaves Denham's job and is rehired by printer Keimer.
- Has an affair that results in the birth of his illegitimate son William in 1729.
- Helps establish the Junto, a society of young men meeting for self-improvement, study, mutual aid, and conviviality.

**1728**

- Establishes a Philadelphia printing partnership with Hugh Meredith in June and rents a building for a home and print shop.
- Composes *Articles of Belief and Acts of Religion.*
- Deborah Read's husband John Rogers runs away from Philadelphia.

**1729**

- Writes a pamphlet titled *The Nature and Necessity of a Paper Currency.*
- Purchases *The Pennsylvania Gazette* from Samuel Keimer.

**1730**

- Elected the official printer for Pennsylvania.
- Takes a common-law wife, Deborah Read Rogers, on September 1.
- Buys out his printing partner, Hugh Meredith.
- Starts agitating for fire protection programs after a fire destroys part of Philadelphia.

## 1731

- Joins the St. John's Freemasons Lodge.
- Draws up the Library Company's articles of association on July 1, founding the first lending library in the country.
- Sponsors his journeyman Thomas Whitmarsh as a printing partner in South Carolina.
- Rents commercial space to his mother-in-law, who sells her well-known ointment.
- Prints an article in *The Gazette* on the imminent passage of the "mortifying" Molasses Act.

## 1732

- Birth of his son Francis Folger.
- Starts printing America's first German-language newspaper, *Philadelphische Zeitung*, which soon fails.
- Publishes the first edition of *Poor Richard's Almanack* on December 28.

## 1733

- Francis Folger Franklin is baptized at the Anglican Christ Church.

## 1734

- Elected Grand Master of the Grand Masonic Lodge of Masons of Philadelphia.
- Buys property on Philadelphia's Market Street.
- Bribes post riders to carry his Philadelphia Gazette after Postmaster Andrew Bradford forbids it.

## 1735

- Brother James Franklin dies; Benjamin sends his widow 500 copies of *Poor Richard* for free.

- Andrew Hamilton defends John Peter Zenger in a seminal Freedom of the Press case.

## 1736

- Named Clerk of the Philadelphia Assembly.
- Prints currency for NJ.
- Son Francis (Franky) Folger dies at age four of smallpox.
- Organizes the Union Fire Company.
- Prints *A Treaty of Friendship held with the Chiefs of the Six Nations at Philadelphia*.
- Oversees the first public use of the Philadelphia State House (Independence Hall).

## 1737

- Appointed Postmaster of Philadelphia.

## 1739

- Benjamin's house is robbed.
- George Whitefield, the Great Awakening preacher, arrives in Philadelphia.
- Leads an environmental protest against polluting industries near the public docks and streets.

## 1740

- Becomes the official printer for New Jersey.
- Prints much material for George Whitefield.
- Advertises the "Franklin Stove."
- Publishes the first edition of *The General Magazine and Historical Chronicle*.

## 1742

- Organizes and publicizes a project to sponsor plant collecting trips by John Bartram.

**1743**

- Attends Archibald Spencer's Boston lectures on natural philosophy.
- Publishes *A Proposal for Promoting Useful Knowledge,* leading to the founding of the American Philosophical Society.
- Daughter Sally is born and baptized at Christ Church.

**1744**

- The American Philosophical Society begins meeting.

**1745**

- Death of Josiah Franklin, Benjamin's father.

**1746**

- Begins extensive electrical experiments.
- Peter Collinson sends Benjamin an electric tube.

**1747**

- Writes *The Plain Truth*, a pamphlet arguing for better military preparedness in Philadelphia.
- Publishes the first political cartoon in America.
- Becomes deeply engrossed in the study of electricity.

**1748**

- Joins the Philadelphia militia after turning down a commission as a Colonel due to military inexperience.

**1749**

- Presents his vision for education in a pamphlet titled *Publick Academy of Philadelphia,* leading to the founding of the University of Pennsylvania.

**1751**

- Letters on electricity are published in London by Peter Collinson.

**1752**

- Conducts the kite experiment.
- Receives the Copley Medal from the Royal Society of London for research in electricity.
- Appointed Deputy Postmaster General of North America.
- Writes a plan for a union of the colonies for security and defense.
- Helps found the Philadelphia Contributionship for Insuring of Houses from Loss by Fire.

**1753**

- Receives honorary degrees from Harvard and Yale.
- Appointed joint Deputy Postmaster General of North America.

**1754**

- Proposes a plan of colonial union at the Albany Congress.

**1757-1762**

- Serves as agent for the Pennsylvania Assembly, and later for Massachusetts, Georgia, and New Jersey in England.

**1759**

- Receives an honorary degree of Doctor of Laws from the University of St. Andrews, Scotland.

**1762**

- Maps postal routes in the colonies.
- Invents the glass armonica.

**1764-1765**

- Charts the Gulf Stream.

**1766**

- Examined in the House of Commons in support of repealing the Stamp Act.

**1768**

- Named Colonial Agent for Georgia.

**1769**

- Named Colonial Agent for New Jersey.

**1770**

- Elected Colonial Agent for Massachusetts.

**1771**

- Tours Ireland.

**1771-1772**

- Begins writing his autobiography.

**1774**

- Dressed down before London's Privy Council by Solicitor

General Wedderburn for leaking letters in the "Hutchinson Affair."
- His wife, Deborah Read, dies in Philadelphia.

## 1775

- Elected as a Pennsylvania delegate to the Second Continental Congress.
- Serves as chairman of the Pennsylvania Committee of Safety.
- Elected Postmaster General of the Colonies.

## 1776

- Presides over the Constitutional Convention of Philadelphia.
- Serves on a committee of five to draft the Declaration of Independence.
- Arrives in Paris on December 21 as one of the Commissioners of Congress to the French Court.

## 1777

- Meets Madame Brillon, an amour.

## 1778

- Signs the French Alliance.

## 1779-1781

- Appointed to negotiate the peace treaty with England.

## 1780

- Madame Helvetius rejects Benjamin's offer of marriage.

**1783-1784**

- Signs the Peace Treaty.
- Invents bifocals.

**1785-1786**

- Elected President of the Pennsylvania Executive Council.
- Invents the "long arm" for retrieving books from high shelves.

**1787**

- Signs the United States Constitution.

**1789**

- Writes an anti-slavery treatise.
- Becomes president of the Society for Promoting the Abolition of Slavery.

**1790**

- April 17: Dies in Philadelphia at the age of eighty-four. His funeral at Philadelphia's Christ Church Burial Ground is attended by 20,000 mourners.

## B. Fun Facts About Ben Franklin

- Early Vegetarianism: At the age of sixteen, Benjamin adopted a vegetarian lifestyle while apprenticing at a print shop, inspired by a book by early vegetarian advocate Thomas Tryon. He was also influenced by the moral arguments of prominent vegetarian Quakers in colonial Pennsylvania, such as Benjamin Lay and John Woolman. His reasons for choosing vegetarianism were rooted in health, ethics, and economy. Though, later in life he started incorporating fish in his diet.

- Musical Talents: Ben played several instruments, including the violin, harp, and guitar. He even made his own glass armonica, which he played by touching the edge of the spinning glass with damp fingers.

- First Volunteer Fire Company: In 1736, Ben started the first volunteer fire company in Philadelphia, demonstrating his commitment to public service.

- Birthdate Confusion: Although Ben is arguably Philadelphia's most famous resident, he was born in Boston on January 6, 1706. Due to the switch from the Julian to the Gregorian calendar in 1752, which corrected the calendar year by removing eleven days to better align with the solar year, his birthday changed to January 17. It remains unknown how Ben chose to celebrate his birthday.

- Early Aspirations: Ben wanted to be a sailor, but his father, who had lost an older son at sea, directed him to learn the printing business from his older brother. Ben later opened a print shop and published the *Pennsylvania Gazette* and *Poor Richard's Almanack*. He established the first commercial franchise system in the Americas by expanding his print shop to other colonies.

- Postal Service Contributions: Ben served as postmaster of Philadelphia and co-deputy postmaster of British North America. In 1775, he became the first postmaster general of the United States.

- Innovative Swimmer: At age eleven, Ben invented a pair of swim fins for his hands and was inducted into the International Swimming Hall of Fame in 1968 for his contributions to the sport.

- Franklin Stove: Ben invented the Franklin stove, an iron furnace that used less wood than other furnaces of the time, improving heating efficiency.

- Bifocal Lenses: As his vision worsened with age, Ben invented bifocals by combining lenses that allowed him to see both close up and far away.

- Pseudonymous Writer: Ben wrote under several pseudonyms, including Silence Dogood, Polly Baker, and Richard Saunders.

- Gulf Stream Discovery: Ben is credited with discovering the Gulf Stream.

- Family Life: Ben had three children and eight grandchildren.

- Founding Document Signer: Ben is the only person in history to have signed all four documents that helped create the US:

    1. The Declaration of Independence.
    2. The Treaty of Alliance, Amity, and Commerce with France.
    3. The Treaty of Peace between England, France, and the US.
    4. The US Constitution.

- American Philosophical Society: In 1744, Ben founded the American Philosophical Society, promoting knowledge and scientific inquiry.

- Lightning and Electricity: While Ben didn't discover electricity, he proved that lightning and electricity are connected through his famous kite experiment.

- Misquotes: Ben is often misquoted. The phrase "A penny saved is a penny earned" is attributed to him, but he actually wrote in the 1737 *Poor Richard's Almanack* "A penny saved is twopence clear."

- Hospital Founder: In the 1750s, Ben helped found the first hospital in the colonies, Pennsylvania Hospital, which still operates today in Philadelphia.

- Autobiography: Ben wrote an autobiography, the first of its kind to achieve widespread attention, which was published posthumously in 1790.

## C. Selected Letters and Writings

### Notable Writings

1. *Poor Richard's Almanack* (1732–1758): A yearly almanac published under the pseudonym Richard Saunders, known for its aphorisms and proverbs.

2. *The Pennsylvania Gazette* (1729–1766): A newspaper published by Benjamin, which became one of the most successful in the colonies.

3. *Autobiography of Benjamin Franklin* (1771–1790): An unfinished record of his life and achievements, offering insights into his thoughts and philosophies.

4. *Silence Dogood Letters* (1722): A series of satirical letters published in *The New-England Courant* under the pseudonym Silence Dogood.

5. *A Dissertation on Liberty and Necessity, Pleasure and Pain* (1725): A philosophical pamphlet discussing determinism and free will.

6. *The Way to Wealth* (1758): An essay composed of adages and advice, originally published in *Poor Richard's Almanack*.

7. *Experiments and Observations on Electricity* (1751–1753): A collection of letters and scientific papers documenting his experiments with electricity.

8. *The Morals of Chess* (1786): An essay praising chess and prescribing a code of conduct for the game.

9. *Observations Concerning the Increase of Mankind, Peopling of Countries, etc.* (1751): An essay on demographics and the growth of the American colonies.

10. *An Edict by the King of Prussia* (1773): A satirical piece criticizing British colonial policies by pretending to be an edict from the King of Prussia.

Notable Letters

1. Letters to the Royal Society (1750-1753): Correspondence discussing his experiments with electricity and other scientific inquiries.

2. Letter to Lord Kames (1767): Correspondence discussing philosophical ideas and personal reflections.

3. Letter to Joseph Priestley (1772): A letter to the noted chemist discussing scientific discoveries and theories.

4. Letters to William Strahan (1765–1775): Correspondence with his friend and British printer, reflecting on politics and personal matters.

5. Letters to Sarah Bache (1771–1788): Letters to his daughter, discussing family matters and offering paternal advice.

6. Letters to William Franklin (1762–1784): Correspondence with his son, covering topics from personal advice to political disagreements.

7. Letter to Jean-Baptiste Le Roy (1785): Discussing his views on life, science, and philosophical matters.

8. Letter to the Rev. George Whitefield (1752): Correspondence with the prominent preacher, discussing religion and personal beliefs.

9. Letter to Ezra Stiles (1790): A letter in which Benjamin discusses his religious beliefs near the end of his life.

10. Letter to the Committee of Secret Correspondence (1776): A letter regarding his diplomatic mission to France during the American Revolution.

## D. Famous Quotes by Benjamin Franklin

1. "Wish not so much to live long as to live well."
− Benjamin Franklin, Poor Richard's Almanack

2. "He does not possess wealth; it possesses him."
− Benjamin Franklin, Poor Richard's Almanack

3. "There are no gains, without pain."
− Benjamin Franklin, Poor Richard's Almanack

4. "In reality, there is, perhaps, no one of our natural passions so hard to subdue as pride."
− Benjamin Franklin, Autobiography Collection: Henry Ford, Nikola Tesla, and Benjamin Franklin

5. "It is better to take many injuries than to give one."
− Benjamin Franklin, Poor Richard's Almanack

6. "If you would not be forgotten as soon as you are dead and rotten, either write things worth reading, or do things worth the writing."
− Benjamin Franklin, Poor Richard's Almanack

7. "Lost time is never found again."
− Benjamin Franklin, Poor Richard's Almanack

8. "Human felicity is produced not so much by great pieces of good fortune that seldom happen, as by little advantages that occur every day."
− Benjamin Franklin, Autobiography Collection: Henry Ford, Nikola Tesla, and Benjamin Franklin

9. "Content makes poor men rich; discontent makes rich men poor."
− Benjamin Franklin, Poor Richard's Almanack

10. "Haste makes waste."
— Benjamin Franklin, Poor Richard's Almanack

11. "Don't throw stones at your neighbors, if your own windows are glass."
— Benjamin Franklin, Poor Richard's Almanack

12. "For life is a kind of chess, in which we often have points to gain, and competitors or adversaries to contend with, and in which there is a vast variety of good and ill events, that are, in some degree, the effect of prudence, or the want of it."
— Benjamin Franklin, The Morals of Chess

13. "Fools need advice most, but wise men only are the better for it."
— Benjamin Franklin, Poor Richard's Almanack

14. "A true friend is the best possession."
— Benjamin Franklin, Poor Richard's Almanack

15. "He that's content, hath enough; He that complains, has too much."
— Benjamin Franklin, Poor Richard's Almanack

16. "So convenient a thing is it to be a reasonable creature, since it enables one to find or make a reason for everything one has a mind to do."
— Benjamin Franklin, Autobiography Collection: Henry Ford, Nikola Tesla, and Benjamin Franklin

17. "Early to bed and early to rise, makes a man healthy, wealthy, and wise."
— Benjamin Franklin, Poor Richard's Almanack

18. "Do you love life? Then do not squander time, for that is the stuff life is made of."
— Benjamin Franklin, Poor Richard's Almanack

19. "Don't value a man for the quality he is of, but for the qualities he possesses."
— Benjamin Franklin, Poor Richard's Almanack

20. "Great modesty often hides great merit."
— Benjamin Franklin, Poor Richard's Almanack

21. "As we enjoy great advantages from the inventions of others, we should be glad of an opportunity to serve others by any invention of ours, and this we should do freely and generously."
— Benjamin Franklin, Autobiography Collection: Henry Ford, Nikola Tesla, and Benjamin Franklin

22. "Having been poor is no shame, but being ashamed of it is."
— Benjamin Franklin, Poor Richard's Almanack

23. "Who is strong? He that can conquer his bad habits."
— Benjamin Franklin, Poor Richard's Almanack

24. "Nothing was useful which was not honest."
— Benjamin Franklin, Autobiography Collection: Henry Ford, Nikola Tesla, and Benjamin Franklin

25. "Would you live with ease, do what you ought, and not what you please."
— Benjamin Franklin, Poor Richard's Almanack

26. "I grew convinced that truth, sincerity and integrity in dealings between man and man were of the utmost importance to the felicity of life."
— Benjamin Franklin, Autobiography Collection: Henry Ford, Nikola Tesla, and Benjamin Franklin

27. "Search others for their virtues, thyself for thy vices."
— Benjamin Franklin, Poor Richard's Almanack

28. "What more valuable than Gold? Diamonds. Than diamonds? Virtue."
– Benjamin Franklin, Poor Richard's Almanack

29. "Speak little, do much."
– Benjamin Franklin, Poor Richard's Almanack

30. "When you are good to others, you are best to yourself."
– Benjamin Franklin, Poor Richard's Almanack

31. "Sell not virtue to purchase wealth, nor liberty to purchase power."
– Benjamin Franklin, Poor Richard's Almanack

32. "Those who would give up essential liberty, to purchase a little temporary safety, deserve neither liberty nor safety."
– Benjamin Franklin, Benjamin Franklin: An American Life by Walter Isaacson

33. "Rebellion to tyrants is obedience to God."
– Benjamin Franklin, Benjamin Franklin: An American Life by Walter Isaacson

34. "Without freedom of thought there can be no such thing as wisdom; and no such thing as public liberty, without freedom of speech."
– Benjamin Franklin, Benjamin Franklin: An American Life by Walter Isaacson

35. "The way to see by faith is to shut the eye of reason."
– Benjamin Franklin, Poor Richard's Almanack

36. "He's a fool that makes his doctor his heir."
– Benjamin Franklin, Poor Richard's Almanack

37. "Teach your child to hold his tongue; he'll learn fast enough to speak."
– Benjamin Franklin, Poor Richard's Almanack

38. "Visits should be short, like a winter's day, lest you're too troublesome to hasten away."
– Benjamin Franklin, Poor Richard's Almanack

39. "It was about this time I conceived the bold and arduous project of arriving at moral perfection... I soon found I had undertaken a task of more difficulty than I had imagined."
– Benjamin Franklin, Autobiography Collection: Henry Ford, Nikola Tesla, and Benjamin Franklin

40. "Love your Enemies, for they tell you your faults."
– Benjamin Franklin, Poor Richard's Almanack

41. "The poor have little, beggars none, the rich too much, enough not one."
– Benjamin Franklin, Poor Richard's Almanack

42. "To lengthen thy life, lessen thy meals."
– Benjamin Franklin, Poor Richard's Almanack

43. "Better slip with your feet than tongue."
– Benjamin Franklin, Poor Richard's Almanack

44. "A man being sometimes more generous when he has but a little money than when he has plenty, perhaps thro' fear of being thought to have but little."
– Benjamin Franklin, Autobiography Collection: Henry Ford, Nikola Tesla, and Benjamin Franklin

45. "He that lies down with dogs shall rise up with fleas."
– Benjamin Franklin, Poor Richard's Almanack

46. "Reading was the only amusement I allowed myself."
– Benjamin Franklin, Autobiography Collection: Henry Ford, Nikola Tesla, and Benjamin Franklin

# References

Baracskay, Daniel. *Benjamin Franklin.* Free Speech Center (2024). https://firstamendment.mtsu.edu/article/benjamin-franklin/. Accessed July 09, 2024

Brindell Fradin, Dennis. *Who Was Ben Franklin?* New York. Grosset & Dunlap, 2002.

Fleming, Thomas. *Ben Franklin: Inventing America.* Minnesota. Quarto Publishing Group, 2016.

Franklin, Benjamin. *Autobiography of Benjamin Franklin.* New York. Harper & Brothers, 1849.

Isaacson, Walter. *Benjamin Franklin: An American Life.* New York. Simon & Schuster, 2004.

Weiner, Eric. *Ben Franklin: The US Founding Father who travelled the globe.* BBC (2024). https://www.bbc.com/travel/article/20240513-ben-franklin-the-us-founding-father-who-travelled-the-globe. Accessed July 11, 2024

Wilkes, Jonny. *Benjamin Franklin: the Founding Father who saved America.* History Extra (2024). https://www.historyextra.com/period/georgian/benjamin-franklin-facts-life-death/. Accessed July 15, 2024

Wood, Gordon S. and Hornberger, Theodore. *Benjamin Franklin: American author, scientist, and statesman.* Britannica (2024). https://www.britannica.com/biography/Benjamin-Franklin. Accessed July 06, 2024

**Thanks for reading!**

As we close the final chapter of *A Brief History of Benjamin Franklin for Kids*, I am grateful for the opportunity to have embarked on this journey with you through the pages of this book. Writing this narrative has been a labor of love, driven by my deep admiration for Franklin's extraordinary life and lasting legacy. Each chapter reflects my commitment to highlighting the intricacies of his story and the profound influence it continues to have on our understanding of innovation, resilience, and civic duty.

This book goes beyond mere historical documentation; it is a heartfelt tribute to Benjamin Franklin's enduring spirit and the timeless significance of his contributions to science, politics, and society. Countless hours of research and reflection have gone into capturing the essence of his experiences, as well as the broader historical context in which they unfolded. Through meticulous attention to detail and narrative nuance, I have endeavored to bring Franklin's world vividly to life, inviting readers to immerse themselves in his journey of ingenuity, curiosity, and entrepreneurial courage.

Your feedback is invaluable to me, serving not only as a reflection of your engagement with the text but also as a guiding light for future readers. Whether you found inspiration in Franklin's brilliance, were moved by his profound reflections, or have suggestions for how this work could be further enriched, I welcome your insights with an open heart and a deep sense of gratitude.

Please take a moment to share your thoughts and reflections by leaving a review. Your voice can shape the collective narrative of Franklin's legacy and inspire others to embark on their own journey of discovery. Simply scan or click the QR code provided, which directs you to the Amazon page where you can leave your review. Your feedback is a vital contribution to our ongoing exploration of history's enduring lessons.

Thank you for joining me on this journey through the life and legacy of Benjamin Franklin. May our shared appreciation for his story serve as a beacon of inspiration and understanding in an ever-changing world.

Warm regards,

Scott Matthews

# FIND MORE OF MY BOOKS ON AMAZON!

# DISCOVER MORE TITLES OF THE SERIES "A BRIEF HISTORY OF ..."!

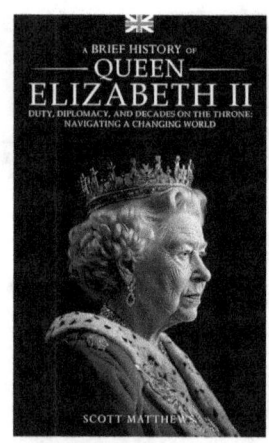

# Explore the "Why Do We Say That" Series and Uncover the Origins of Everyday Idioms and Phrases

**Bonus!**

Thanks for supporting me and purchasing this book! I'd like to send you some freebies. They include:

- The digital version of *500 World War I & II Facts*

- The digital version of *101 Idioms and Phrases*

- The audiobook for my best seller *1144 Random Facts*

Scan the QR code below, enter your email and I'll send you all the files. Happy reading!

www.ingramcontent.com/pod-product-compliance
Lightning Source LLC
Chambersburg PA
CBHW072101110526
44590CB00018B/3267